Let's Both Win

Arnold Mol

Marshalls

Marshalls Paperbacks
Marshall Morgan & Scott
3 Beggarwood Lane, Basingstoke, Hants, RG23 7LP, UK

Copyright © 1981 Femina, Forum Building, Bosman Street, Pretoria.

First published by Femina Publishers.
First published in the U.K. by Marshall Morgan & Scott 1984.

ISBN 0 551 01074 6

Printed and bound in Great Britain by
Anchor Brendon Ltd, Tiptree, Essex

To "Joybells" —
my winning partner

AFTER MARRIAGE

Mrs Sullen: Pray, Spouse, what did you marry for?

Sullen: To get an heir to my estate.

Sir Charles: And have you succeeded?

Sul: No.

Archer: The condition fails of his side. — Pray, Madam, what did you marry for?

Mrs. Sul: To support the weakness of my sex by the strength of his, and to enjoy the pleasures of an agreeable society.

Sir Ch: Are your expectations answered?

Mrs. Sul: No . . .

Sir Ch: What are the bars to your mutual contentment?

Mrs. Sul: In the first place, I can't drink ale with him.

Sul: Nor can I drink tea with her.

Mrs. Sul: I can't hunt with you.

Sul: Nor can I dance with you.

Mrs. Sul: I hate cocking and racing.

Sul: And I abhor ombre and piquet.

Mrs. Sul: Your silence is intolerable.

Sul: Your prating is worse.

Mrs. Sul: Have we not been a perpetual offence to each other — a gnawing vulture at the heart?

Sul: A frightful goblin to the sight.

Mrs. Sul: A porcupine to the feeling.

Sul: Perpetual wormwood to the taste.

Mrs. Sul: Is there on earth a thing we could agree in?

Sul: Yes — to part.

Mrs. Sul: With all my heart.

GEORGE FARQUHAR. *The Beaux's Stratagem.* 1707

Contents

Foreword

The escalating disintegration of marriage all over the world poses a very real danger to a healthy family life and ultimately to society. Families are the building bricks of society. Weak and crumbling bricks can only lead to unsafe houses and the analogy serves to illustrate one of the greatest threats to Western civilization. Never before in our history has the family as a unit been so under attack from the spiritual and social forces of destruction. But God's binding force for preserving family unity, is marriage. Healthy partnerships produce healthy, strong families.

No one in his or her right mind will attempt a totally new task without *some* measure of preparation. A housewife will not even switch on her new washing machine without first reading the accompanying handbook. Yet countless couples move or rush into marriage without study or guidance and matrimony, after all, is infinitely more precious *and* complex than a washing machine. The careful reading of a book like the one you are holding right now will certainly bring this point home. For instance, how many partners realize that when they are joined together as husband and wife *an individually definable role* is given, and these roles can be fulfilled in what is called the marriage function. Because Arnold Mol's excellent book deals essentially with the function, a few words about rôle will be appropriate here. In Christian context, we could well replace the term rôle by *calling* and function by *task*.

A *husband's call* can be described by the term *overall responsibility*. It is not determined by his personality, background, education, finances or circumstances, but simply by the fact that he is the male partner. He has the overall responsibility for the emotional, intellectual, material and spiritual welfare of his family. In the very task of marriage, husband and wife will share the actual duties of training and guiding the children's religious beliefs, but the father holds the final responsibility.

The *wife's call* can be described as that of the *support system*. This call is by no means inferior, but *complimentary*. By way of illustration, let us look at soldiers on the battlefront. They are called to destroy the enemy but at the same time they are dependent on a vast support system. Transport, medical services, food supplies, ammunition supplies etc., are vital. A soldier can accomplish little without the support system and the latter is rather purposeless without the former. They are complimentary. A rundown support system isn't much of a help on the battlefront and wives who are allowed to become rundown are hardly the ideal help to their husbands.

All this may sound rather biblical and old-fashioned, but He who designed mankind and instituted marriage surely knows best how mankind in general, and marriage and families in particular, should operate. We can only be the better off for heeding His guidance in these matters. The non-acceptance of the call and the subsequent confusion of sexual roles, further aggravated by a highly pressurised society, lie at the heart of so many problems. On the other hand, understanding and wholehearted acceptance of the respective calls lead to a dynamic and enthusiastic approach to the development of the marriage task.

Finally, something about the author of this book. I have known Arnold Mol for some twenty years — as a teenager, student, and married man. Our acquaintance was, and still is, a pleasure. Devotion, intelligence, compassion and a sense of humour are the sort of ingredients that make up a whole person, well capable of writing this timely and highly informative book.

Dr Louw Alberts
President: National Institute For Metallurgy

Part 1:
Sources of conflict

We are not unique

What happened to the moonlight and roses?

Almost every couple enters into marriage with the determination that "ours is going to be different". They are determined to avoid the pitfalls and the problems that they see in so many other marriages. They are determined that the romantic excitement of their courtship is not going to fade.

But for most couples it does. As they settle down after the honeymoon their relationship changes and they become aware of friction. They get annoyed with one another every now and then. They begin to argue about issues over which they thought they would never disagree. The glow and the thrill of their love seems to be diminishing and they wonder why things are going wrong. Some begin to have doubts. Did they make a mistake? Did they choose the wrong partner?

Conflict is a natural part of marriage

For some couples these problems crop up quite early in their marriage — for others it comes later on. But sooner or later every couple experiences conflict. Every couple experiences problems that threaten the closeness of their relationship. Such conflict is not extraordinary — it is a natural part of marriage. In fact the couple who does *not* experience such conflict may be considered to be unique.

When two individuals become interdependent — living together, deciding together, sleeping together — their relationship will be exposed to all kinds of stresses and strains. Several times I have said to my wife that I have sometimes regretted getting married but that I have never regretted marrying her. What I was trying to say was that the reason for our conflict was not that there was something wrong with my wife but that conflict was an inevitable part of the marriage.

Why all this conflict?

There are several reasons for conflict's being a natural part of

13

marriage. Although these may differ from couple to couple, we can cite four major reasons

1. Differences in temperament
2. The problem of making decisions together
3. The natural decline in communication
4. The wife's desire to dominate her husband and the husband's desire to rule over her.

Differences in temperament

We are all individuals. We all have strengths and we all have weaknesses. We view situations differently from others. We think differently. We react differently. We behave differently. That's what makes our lives rich and varied. When two individuals join their lives there is rarely a perfect fit. Adjustment is necessary — a corner to be rounded off here or a rough edge to be smoothed over there — hence friction of one kind or another is inevitable. In part two we will take a closer look at the various temperaments: what they are like; how they influence our behaviour, particularly in the marriage relationship; and, above all, how we can adjust to them.

The problem of making decisions together

When we are single we can make decisions on our own without having to consult anyone else. We have the final say. But marriage changes all this. Suddenly our partners have an equal say. Their views and their tastes must be considered — and because we are all individuals, we will always have differences of opinion. Nobody wants to be married to a human vegetable. We all want partners who can think for themselves, who have some backbone, who have some very definite views — and then, of course, we must expect problems when we have to make decisions together! What type of furniture? Where will we live? What colour should the carpet be? What do we do with our money? and so on ...

The issue is not that we *have* differences of opinion but *how we handle* them. Part three will deal with the different styles of decision-making and of handling conflict as well as provide some useful guidelines to developing a constructive way of making decisions.

A natural decline in communication

One of the most exciting aspects of a courtship is the wide range and the depth of communication between two people. The sheer wonder of discovering one another — of sharing common views, of stimulating one another's thinking. Yet this too, seems to disappear. Couples who used to sit up talking into the small hours now rarely take the time to communicate their innermost feelings to one another. There just seems to be a natural decline in the level of communication.

In part four we will explore the various levels of communication. We will identify the barriers that prevent intimate communication between husband and wife and also give some hints on improving the quality of communication.

Inherent inclinations

It may come as quite a shock to you to know that when Adam and Eve sinned, God cursed, among other things, the marriage relationship. He had intended them to have a partnership on an equal footing where each one fulfilled a specific function. However, when sin marred the relationship, God told the woman that she would give birth to children with pain and that "Your desire will be for your husband and he will rule over you." (Genesis 3:16.)

What does "her desire will be for her husband" mean? The word "desire" does not mean loving affection here for the only other time Moses used this particular word was in Genesis 4:7 where God said to Cain, "Sin is crouching at your door; it desires to have you, but you must master it." Now we know that sin does not have a loving affection, but rather a desire to control and dominate us.

So what the curse on the woman actually implied was that she would want to control her husband, and that in response he would rule over her. Here is the origin of the "battle of the sexes", "women's lib" and male chauvinism. Conflict is inevitable whenever a wife tries to dominate her husband or whenever a husband lords it over his wife.

In part five we will discuss how lasting happiness is achieved in marriage: when husband and wife relate to each other in quite the opposite way to the curse's prescription.

Marriage is hard work

No relationship can continue indefinitely, let alone grow if it is not consciously worked on. Only people in fairy tales get married and "live happily ever after" — in real life we have to build our relationship with purposeful determination particularly since there are so many "natural" forces which cause conflict and erode the relationship.

The main purpose of this book is to show that, although conflict in marriage is very common, it can not only be *understood* but also *overcome*. Marriage can be "heaven on earth" even for a couple who seem to be extreme opposites. My wife Joy and I are such a couple. We are such opposites in so many ways and we experienced a great deal of conflict in the early years of our marriage. But we have developed a relationship which has enriched every facet of our lives and brought out the best in both of us. But we had to work hard at it, and are still working hard at it, because we still have a long way to grow.

A coquette is a being who wishes to please. Amiable being! If you do not like her, you will have no difficulty in finding a female companion of a different mood. Alas! coquettes are but too rare. 'Tis a career that requires great abilities, infinite pains, a gay and airy spirit. 'Tis the coquette that provides all amusement ... She is the stirring element amid the heavy congeries of social atoms; the soul of the house, the salt of the banquet.

BENJAMIN DISRAELI, EARL OF BEACONSFIELD
Coningsby, 1844

Part 2:
Differences in
temperament

That's typically you

You never ... you always ...

Charlotte was battling to come out on her small housekeeping allowance. When she found out that Frank had impulsively bought an expensive watch for a friend, she blew her top. "You *never* think of me and the baby. You *always* do more for your friends than you do for us." Frank was deeply hurt that she did not think his generosity praiseworthy.

George found Emily crying her eyes out because she had not been invited to a friend's tea-party. George told her not to be stupid. Such tea-parties were a waste of time, anyway. She shouldn't *always* take such things as a personal insult. Emily sulked for the rest of the evening, telling George that he *never* had any sympathy for her.

Peter came home from work and asked Betty what time supper would be served. She replied, "You *always* expect far too much from me. I've had a terrible day, and I just can't have supper ready on time." Peter wanted to know why she *always* saw every question as a personal criticism. He was upset because Betty blamed him. "Why can't she *ever* answer a straight-forward question?" he wondered.

Janet told Dick that their 9-year old son had been spanked unfairly at school by a teacher who was known to lose his temper frequently. Dick sighed from behind his newspaper and said, "Why doesn't one of the parents go and see the principal?" Janet retorted angrily, "You *never* want to get involved in anything. You *always* leave it to someone else." She was angry for the rest of the day.

We're made differently

Each of these couples was experiencing conflict because of their differences in temperament.

Charlotte is an anxious person, while Frank is impulsive. Emily is easily offended, while George is unsympathetic. Peter is naive, while Betty is a perfectionist. Dick is passive, while Janet gets angry quickly.

Although each person is unique, has a distinct, individual

character and nobody is *exactly* like another person, we can nevertheless describe general patterns of behaviour. There are numerous ways of classifying temperament but the most common one stems from the ancient Greeks. Hippocrates suggested that there were four basic temperaments, depending on the kind of fluid which flowed through a person's veins

— if you had mainly *warm blood* flowing through your veins you had a *sanguine* temperament
— if you had *yellow bile* as the dominant fluid you had a *choleric* temperament
— if you had *black bile* you had a *melancholy* temperament, and
— if your veins were predominantly filled with *phlegm* you had a *phlegmatic* temperament.

Today we know that one's temperament is not determined by body fluids. However, the four categories are still useful ways of describing different temperaments.

Before you read any further it may be fun for you to answer the questions in the Temperament Inventory in order to determine your predominant temperament.

Temperament Inventory

Here are some questions about the way you think, feel and behave in different situations. Next to each question is a space for answering "yes", "no" or "?" (meaning "I don't know" or "sometimes"). Decide what is your *usual* way of acting or feeling when you are alone, or in the presence of your partner and/or immediate members of your family. Mark your answer accordingly.

Work *quickly* and don't spend too much time over any one question. Your *first reaction* is more important than a long drawn-out thought process.

Try to answer "yes" or "no" as often as possible. Mark the ?-answer *only* when you are really not sure, or when the truth is definitely somewhere in between.

N.B. It may be a good idea to write your answers on a separate piece of paper so that your mate can also answer the questions without seeing *your* answers.

Make sure that you answer *every* question and remember that there are no right or wrong answers. This is not a test of ability but simply a pointer to the way *you* think, feel and behave.

1. Do you *normally* eat faster than other people even when there is no reason to hurry?   Yes ? No

2. When people give you a compliment, do you *generally* believe them?   Yes ? No

3. Would you *generally* prefer to stay at home and do your own thing, rather than go out visiting friends?   Yes ? No

4. Do you *sometimes* feel that you don't care what happens to you?

5. When catching a train or a bus, do you *often* arrive at the last minute?   Yes ? No

6. Are you *usually* easy-going — not easily agitated?   Yes ? No

7. Do you *usually* think carefully before deciding anything?   Yes ? No

8. Do you become irritated *quickly* when things are not in their proper places?   Yes ? No

9. Do you *often* gesticulate with your hands when you talk?   Yes ? No

10. Do you find it *relatively* easy to keep your emotions under control?   Yes ? No

11. Are you *often* suspicious of other people's motives?   Yes ? No

12. Do you *frequently* feel that people frown upon the things that you say and do?   Yes ? No

13. When driving a car, do you *often* get frustrated in slow-moving traffic?   Yes ? No

14. Are you *on the whole* satisfied with your physical appearance?   Yes ? No

15. Do you *normally* find it difficult to go up to strangers at a social gathering and introduce yourself?   Yes ? No

16. Do you *often* feel restless as though you're looking for something but you're not sure what?   Yes ? No

17. Do people who drive very cautiously *generally* get on your nerves?   Yes ? No

18. Do you *usually* make up your own mind regardless of what other people might

think of your decision? Yes ? No

19. When you want to buy an expensive article, can you *normally* save up for it patiently? Yes ? No

20. Do you have some bad habits that you *sometimes* feel you ought to have discarded long ago? Yes ? No

21. Do other people *usually* know what you are thinking and feeling? Yes ? No

22. Would you say that *on the whole* you are satisfied with your life up to now? Yes ? No

23. Do you plan *most* of your activities well ahead of time? Yes ? No

24. Do you *generally* spend a good deal of time worrying over financial matters? Yes ? No

25. Do you *usually* show your impatience when someone has kept you waiting? Yes ? No

26. When you feel downhearted do you *normally* try to find someone to cheer you up? Yes ? No

27. Would you *generally* prefer to see a documentary rather than a comedy on TV? Yes ? No

28. Are you *frequently* bothered by a guilty conscience? Yes ? No

29. Do you *often* find yourself crossing a busy street, leaving your more careful companions on the other side? Yes ? No

30. When you have made a social blunder can you *normally* forget about it quite easily? Yes ? No

31. Would you *generally* keep your opinions to yourself if you thought it might upset someone who was present? Yes ? No

32. When you see a picture on the wall hanging obliquely, do you *usually* have difficulty in concentrating until it has been put straight? Yes ? No

33. Do you think it pointless to analyse your own thoughts and feelings *regularly*? Yes ? No

34. Do you *usually* have specific goals and a definite sense of direction in your life?   Yes   ?   No

35. If someone in a social group expresses a point of view that differs from yours, would you *normally* keep quiet rather than tell them that you disagree?   Yes   ?   No

36. Do you *often* feel that there isn't much in your life that you can be proud of?   Yes   ?   No

37. Are you *usually* very talkative when you are with people whom you know?   Yes   ?   No

38. Do you *generally* feel that your life is useful and contributes to society?   Yes   ?   No

39. When buying an electrical appliance, do you *usually* read the guarantee before making the purchase?   Yes   ?   No

40. Do you *frequently* prefer to do a task yourself rather than to delegate it to someone else — for fear that they might not do it as well as you would?   Yes   ?   No

41. Do you *often* say and do things on the spur of the moment?   Yes   ?   No

42. When you have done something wrong, can you *normally* forget about it quickly and focus on the future?   *Yes*   ?   *No*

43. Are you *generally* inclined to be deliberate and unhurried in your actions?   Yes   ?   No

44. Do you *at times* keep quiet for fear that people might criticise or laugh at your point of view?   Yes   ?   No

45. Do you *often* tell jokes and funny stories to your friends?   Yes   ?   No

46. Does your future *on the whole* seem promising and bright to you?   Yes   ?   No

47. Do you *frequently* think about your past and the course that your life is taking?   Yes   ?   No

48. After you have completed an important task do you *often* feel that you should have done it better?   Yes   ?   No

Scoring the inventory

— E-A Score 2 points for every *"yes"* answer and 1 point for every *"?"* answer on each of the following questions 1, 5, 9, 13, 17, 21, 25, 29, 33, 37, 41, 45 ☐
— E-B Score 2 points for every *"no"* answer and 1 point for every *"?"* answer on each of the following questions 3, 7, 11, 15, 19, 23, 27, 31, 35, 39, 43, 47 ☐

Add the E-A and E-B scores together for the *Extravert* score

— U-A Score 2 points for every *"yes"* answer and 1 point for every *"?"* answer for each of the following questions 2, 6, 10, 14, 18, 22, 26, 30, 34, 38, 42, 46 ☐
— U-B Score 2 points for every *"no"* answer and 1 point for every *"?"* answer for each of the following questions 4, 8, 12, 16, 20, 24, 28, 32, 36, 40, 44, 48 ☐

Add the U-A and U-B scores together for the *Unemotional* score

Two dimensions of temperament

The four basic temperaments are indicated by a combination of two dimensions viz: introversion-extraversion
emotional-unemotional
Every individual's temperament can be indicated somewhere along the introversion-extraversion scale. The *extreme introvert* is someone who basically lives *inwardly* — he keeps his thoughts and feelings mainly to himself. The *extreme extravert* is someone who basically lives *outwardly* — often expressing his thoughts and feelings.

It is important to note that no person is *either one or the other*. There are degrees of extraversion and introversion. Some people can be more introverted than others — some are more extraverted than others.

Each person's temperament can also be placed somewhere along the emotional-unemotional scale. The *extremely emotional* person will experience a high degree of *emotional fluctuations* — one day they feel on top of the world, the next day they're in the valley of despair. At the other end of the scale we find the *extremely unemotional* person who experiences virtually no *emotional fluctuations*. Such a person very seldom gets upset or despondent about anything — they also rarely get excited about anything.

Again, no person is *either one or the other* — some people are more emotional than others, some are more unemotional than others.

When we draw these two scales at right angles to each other we create four quadrants that represent the four basic temperaments

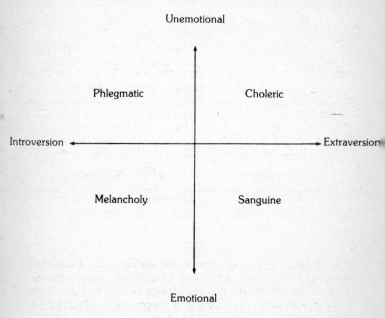

Interpreting your inventory score

Mark your total *extraversion* score on the horizontal axis of the diagram below and your total *unemotional* score on the vertical axis. Draw perpendicular lines to indicate your position with regard to your dominant temperament.

Example: John's extraversion score was 32 and his unemotional score was 9. He therefore has a dominantly sanguine temperament as illustrated on the diagram below

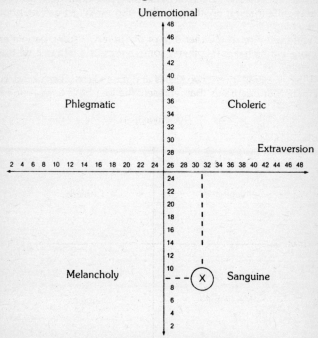

N.B. Results of a questionnaire like this are *suggestive* rather than absolute. Your mood at the time of answering may influence some of your answers. You may therefore find that you have some characteristics that apply to a temperament different from the one indicated on your scoring sheet.

We very seldom come across a "pure" temperament. Most people have a dominant temperament with a good dose of a second temperament thrown in. The closer your temperament position on the above diagram is to one of the axes, the more likely you are to have a mixture of temperaments.

Another reason for finding a discrepancy between your dominant temperament as indicated by the questionnaire, and the characteristics which you think apply to you, is the fact that we do not always see ourselves objectively. A friend of ours who came out as a choleric on the diagram, said that it was not true of her that she expressed her affections in a matter-of-fact manner as most cholerics do. Her husband however, confirmed that she did.

It may therefore be a useful exercise to let your partner answer the questionnaire on your behalf so that you can see yourself as he or she sees you.

Do I have to be me?

Which temperament is the best?

No temperament is better than another one. Each temperament has strengths and each temperament has weaknesses. The characteristics listed below may not *all* apply to *every* person with that temperament, but they are a good representation of the typical strengths and weaknesses.

The Sanguine Temperament

— *Strengths*
Warm-hearted, spontaneous, enthusiastic, sociable, lively, enjoys lots of friends, expresses emotions freely.
— *Weaknesses*
Impulsive, talkative, weak-willed, compromises easily, changes moods rapidly, loves to be the centre of attraction, strong need to be accepted by everyone.

The Choleric Temperament

— *Strengths*
Confident, pioneering, purposeful, strong-willed, self-disciplined, natural leader and organiser.
— *Weaknesses*
Emotionally deficient, unsympathetic, domineering, impatient, self-sufficient, wants things done his way, stubborn.

The Melancholy Temperament

— *Strengths*
Analytical, gifted, creative, self-sacrificing, avoids the limelight, loyal, maintains high standards.

— *Weaknesses*
Introspective, touchy, moody, self-pitying, suspicious, easily angered, pessimistic, indecisive, perfectionist, self-deprecating.

The Phlegmatic Temperament

— *Strengths*
Calm. easy-going. controlled emotions. peacemaker. high stress tolerance. thinks before acting. dry humour. a faithful friend. reliable.
— *Weaknesses*
Lethargic. indecisive. fearful. self-centred. reluctant to become involved. unenthusiastic. unresponsive. sarcastic.

Some familiar characters

The Bible always depicts men as they are. describing both their strengths and their weaknesses. There are four biblical characters who seem to illustrate the four temperaments rather vividly. They are Peter the sanguine. Paul the choleric. Moses the melancholy and Abraham the phlegmatic. In his book. "Transformed Temperaments". Tim La Haye has analysed these characters particularly well.

The most significant thing about their lives is the fact that they all rose to great heights. When they allowed God to take control of their lives He built on their strengths and neutralised their weaknesses.

Sanguine Peter

Peter was extremely *impulsive*. For example. trust a sanguine to invite his friends home while his mother-in-law is sick in bed (Mark 1:29, 30)! When Jesus came walking on the water to the disciples. Peter impulsively asked to do the same. It was only after he had taken a few steps that he realised what he was doing. and started to sink (Matthew 14:28, 29). In the garden of Gethsemane he impulsively drew his sword and cut off the ear of the high priest's servant (John 18:10). while at the lakeside he couldn't wait for the boats to go ashore — he jumped overboard to get to Jesus (John 21:7).

Peter was also very *talkative* — a man with a foot-shaped mouth. On the Mount of Transfiguration he was the only disciple who said anything — and it was obvious that he didn't know what he was talking about (Luke 9:33). When Jesus told his disciples that He was going to die in Jerusalem. Peter immediately told Him that it would not be so (Matthew 16:22) and Jesus rebuked him sharply.

At the trial of Jesus, Peter was accused of being a disciple because they could hear from his *accent* that he was from Galilee (Matthew 6:73). Why did he have to open his mouth? He could have merely warmed himself by the fire, but he was a sanguine who just couldn't stop talking.

Peter was very *self-centred*, often drawing attention to his own virtues (Matthew 19:27, 26:33). His denial of Jesus showed how *weak-willed* he was and how easily he *compromised* his beliefs (Matthew 26:69-74) in order to be *accepted by others*. His *rapidly-changing* moods are indicated by the fact that one minute he was cursing Jesus and the next he was weeping bitterly (Matthew 26:74, 75).

Yet when the Holy Spirit took control of Peter's life, he became a changed man. He spoke *fearlessly* to the crowds as well as to the Jewish Council (Acts 2:14, 4:19, 20). His love of attention made way for *humility*, as he raised Dorcas from the dead without any publicity (Acts 9:40). He accepted Paul's rebuke graciously (Galatians 2:14) after his natural inclination to compromise had momentarily got the better of him. Even in the heat of a discussion Peter was now able to *control his emotions* and not become involved until the end (Acts 15:7).

Peter's life certainly showed that God can use even extreme sanguines for His glory.

Choleric Paul

Paul was extremely *aggressive*, particularly in the way he persecuted the early Christians (Acts 26: 10, 11). He was also extremely *achievement-orientated*. Nothing could prevent him from preaching the gospel, and he endured incredible hardships to achieve this goal (II Corinthians 11:23-28). Even in his writings we can sense his *determination* to press on towards the goal (Philippians 3:14) and his *self-discipline* to keep himself fit for the race (1 Corinthians 9:26, 27).

He was also a *pioneer*, constantly looking for new areas where he could proclaim the good news — unwilling to go where other missionaries had already been (Romans 15:20). He wanted to conquer virgin soil with the gospel. He was simply a *dynamic*

31

leader. Even when he was a prisoner he started giving orders to the Roman soldiers — and they listened to him (Acts 27:20-36). On the other hand, Paul could be very *hard on others*. In Antioch he tore a strip off Peter in front of everybody (Galatians 2:11-14). He refused to take Mark on the second journey because Mark had not completed the first one. Paul was so *unyielding* on this issue that he was even willing to break up his partnership with Barnabas — the man to whom Paul was so indebted (Acts 15:37-39).

He was *self-sufficient* — he provided for his own needs and for those of his travelling companions (Acts 20:34). He even stayed in his own rented house while a prisoner in Rome (Acts 28:30). He was also very *independent* as far as doctrine was concerned. Initially he did not consult the other apostles and even referred somewhat sceptically to "those who seemed to be important" (Galatians 1:16-19 and 2:6). Paul was also *stubborn*. Despite the many warnings he received on the way, he was determined to go to Jerusalem, for no other reason than that he wanted to go (Acts 21:10-14).

The choleric Christian displays less of the fruit of the Spirit (as listed in Galatians 5:22) than any other temperament. Yet again we see how God changed Paul until every fruit of the Spirit — love, joy, peace, gentleness, meekness, faith, kindness, friendliness and self-control was evident in his life. God can certainly use cholerics — He used Paul to give us two-thirds of the New Testament!

Melancholy Moses

Moses was a very *gifted* man. The Bible tells us that he "was educated in all the wisdom of the Egyptians and was powerful in speech and action" (Acts 7:22). Giftedness is a distinct characteristic of the melancholy temperament. Most of the world's artists for example, had melancholy temperaments.

Yet despite his genius Moses was *meek* (Numbers 12:3) and *self-sacrificing* (Exodus 32:31). He did not want to be in the limelight. Hebrews 11:24-27 tells us that he did not want to be known as the son of Pharaoh's daughter, but preferred to be mistreated along with the people of God.

Moses also exhibited some great weaknesses. He was *self-deprecating* — running himself down. In spite of all his abilities he suffered from an *inferiority complex*. That's why he was quite happy to waste all his abilities on tending sheep in the desert. And when God called him, he tried to think of every possible excuse. First he told God that he was not suited for the task (Exodus 3:10, 11). Then he said that he didn't have any theological training (Exodus 3:13). After that he expressed his fear of being rejected (Exodus 4:1) — perhaps thinking of the first time that the Israelites had rejected him 40 years before. Next he claimed that he was not gifted — not eloquent enough (Exodus 4:10). When God countered all his excuses, he made a last attempt to get out of the task (Exodus 4:13) and God became very angry with him.

Running yourself down is not humility. It is an inverted form of pride because it still focuses on self. True humility is to say, "I can do all things through Christ who strengthens me" (Philippians 4:13).

Moses was also a *perfectionist*. He would sit from sunrise to sunset to hear the people's cases — simply because he didn't believe that anybody else could do it as well as he could. It was only when his father-in-law (the first management consultant!) advised him on these matters, that Moses was willing to delegate (Exodus 18:13-18).

He was inclined to become *depressed* (Numbers 11:10-15) and he often became *angry*. For example, he smashed the stone tablets on the ground in his anger. (He was the only man ever to break all ten commandments at once!) His anger made him sin against God (Numbers 20: 3-5, 9-12) and thus he was not allowed to enter the Promised Land.

Yet despite all these weaknesses God formed Moses into *one of the greatest leaders of all history*. God can and does use melancholies, who yield their lives to Him.

Phlegmatic Abraham

Abraham was initially a very *cautious* person, not exhibiting a great deal of faith. God had called him to settle in Canaan but when he got halfway to Haran he settled there, until God had to urge him to move on again (Genesis 11:31).

He found it *difficult to trust God*. As soon as there was a famine in the land, he emigrated to Egypt, and there, to preserve his own life, he was willing to let his wife marry Pharoah (Genesis 12:10-13). When the truth was eventually discovered, he was chased out of Egypt in disgrace — yet he did the very same thing some years later (Genesis 20:11).

Abraham wanted *peace* — at any cost. When his herdsmen started quarrelling with the herdsmen of his nephew Lot, Abraham was prepared to be the least — and even gave up the Promised Land — just for the sake of peace (Genesis 13:7-9).

Because of his *passive* nature he was also *henpecked*. His wife told him to have intercourse with her maid Hagar, yet later she blamed him for this and told him it was all his fault. His only response was to tell her to deal with Hagar as she pleased (Genesis 16:5,6).

But Abraham was a *faithful friend.* When Lot was kidnapped Abraham mustered his men and rescued him, not taking anything for himself in the process, but giving a tenth of the loot to Melchizedek (Genesis 14:14-24). Phlegmatics are extremely *reliable* people once they can be persuaded to accept responsibility, but that does not happen easily. Where a choleric, for example, will see a problem and say, "Let's do something about it" the phlegmatic will ask, "Why doesn't somebody do something about it?" However, Abraham underwent a change. He took the risk and put his trust in God (Genesis 22:12) and so great did his faith become that he was known as "the father of faith" (Romans 4:16-22) and he took his place in God's "Hall of Fame" (Hebrews 11:17-19).

Amazing what God can do with phlegmatics who yield their lives to Him.

Are we stuck with our weaknesses?

The answer is a resounding 'no'. Anyone can change dramatically
   — if you want to change
   — if you know what to change to
   — if you receive encouragement in making the change.

Looking at these four men is ample evidence that when we allow God to take control of our lives, He uses our strengths and He eliminates our weaknesses.

Analysing and understanding your own temperament is therefore *no excuse* whatsoever to indulge your weaknesses. The only reason for taking a closer look at yourself is to do something about the weaknesses and to continue to build on the strengths.

Meanwhile back home ...

Temperament differences in the marriage relationship

How do people with these particular temperaments behave at home? What are they like as marriage partners? How do they express their love? How do they communicate? What happens when decisions have to be made in the home? And of course the ultimate question — do some temperaments make better marriage partners than others? Or are there some temperament combinations that are likely to lead to more successful marriages?
Let's take a closer look at the temperaments in action within the marriage relationship.

The Sanguine Partner

Sanguines usually *express their affections* very freely. They are quite demonstrative and enjoy holding hands and hugging and kissing in public. A phlegmatic partner will consider such a display as totally unnecessary while the melancholy partner will be embarassed for fear of what others might think — yet it is often this spontaneous display of affection that attracted them to the sanguine in the first place. Many a wife longs for her husband to demonstrate his affection more openly, and will often envy the wife of a sanguine husband.
On the other hand sanguines can switch their emotions very quickly, being passionate one minute and annoyed the next. Their partners are often not sure how to handle them, and at times may wonder whether they really mean what they say. There is a real danger that a sanguine's declaration of love may be seen as just another way to gain acceptance and approval from his partner. In other words the focus is on himself rather than on his partner.
Sanguines do a great deal of talking but they seldom *communicate* at a deep level. They love to joke and tell funny stories — but they seldom listen. They can be the life of a party — as long as they are the centre of attraction. A sanguine author had been talking about himself for some time in conversation with

another guest at a cocktail party. Finally he said, "Well, that's enough about me. Let's talk about you. What did you think of my latest book?"

Some sanguines are permanent clowns. They are constantly trying to be funny or to make witty remarks — to such an extent that it is almost impossible to have a serious conversation with them. They frequently do this to avoid any form of intimate communication which they find threatening.

Because of their optimism they seldom identify problems — or don't give them much thought. As a result they find it difficult to understand another person's concern. For example, when their mates express a fear or worry, a typical sanguine comment might be, "Oh! don't let it worry you. Things will turn out all right, you'll see."

When it comes to *decision-making*, the sanguine's impulsiveness really comes to the fore. He is inclined to make snap decisions which are either reversed or regretted later on. Sanguines do not enjoy spending time contemplating issues, and they feel uncomfortable with uncertainty. "Rather a wrong decision than no decision" is often their motto. This can of course create some serious problems in the home, especially when it comes to financial matters. Not only will sanguines buy things on the spur of the moment (they usually cannot refuse a persuasive salesman), but they are also inclined to spend money on friends, often to the dismay of their partners. This is one of the ways they seek to win acceptance and popularity.

Sanguines find it much easier to make promises than to keep them. It's not that they wilfully tell lies. At the time they really mean it. It's just that they are over-optimistic about their ability to keep those promises. As can well be imagined, this can become an endless source of conflict.

The Choleric Partner

Cholerics tend to *express their affection* in a somewhat matter-of-fact way. They usually consider sentimentality to be a sign of weakness and will avoid it as much as possible. At one of our seminars, for example, we had a choleric who stated emphatically that all this business of bringing home flowers was just so much hogwash and that his wife didn't expect anything like that from him. When we asked his wife about this she confirmed that she didn't expect anything like that from him, but that she would absolutely love it if he did bring home something special for her now and then.

On the other hand, cholerics *do* express their affection — they just don't show it in a very sentimental fashion. A husband might ask his choleric wife whether she really loves him, to which she might typically reply, "Of course I do Honey, why do you ask?" Because of their own matter-of-factness they are seldom sensitive to the emotional needs of their partner. They can usually express their love at any moment — since their emotions are not strongly affected by atmosphere and moods.

I have a choleric temperament, while my wife is a melancholy. For example, I find it easy to start hugging her, even at the most inappropriate times, while she is far more dependent on the right atmosphere. She does not welcome my embraces in the kitchen while she is preparing a meal. On the other hand, I can be so involved in a project that for days I don't show my affection — or else I express it in a rather unromantic manner, almost as if I were merely doing my duty.

Cholerics are inclined to be one-way *communicators*. They can present their ideas and thoughts in a very logical and concise manner but generally tend to be poor listeners — especially when it comes to understanding the underlying emotions of their partners. They tend to reason things out in a more objective manner, since they are not plagued by emotional fluctuations. As a result they have great difficulty in responding sensitively to their partner's feelings.

For example, I often present my arguments point for point, i.e. "In the first place ... secondly ... etc." By the time I am through, Joy is unnerved by my methodical point one, point two, point three, etc. and has lost her trend of thought.

Because cholerics often present their ideas in a rather *forceful* manner and seem so sure of themselves, they tend to make others feel inferior even though this is unintentional. The result is that their partners don't feel capable of reasoning with them, and they prefer to keep silent. Unfortunately the communication between them begins to dwindle. On the other hand if their partners do participate in arguments, the relationship is characterised by constant friction and by a battle of wits.

However, the choleric can be identified most clearly in his approach to *decision-making*. Like the sanguine, the choleric also makes quick decisions, but unlike the sanguine, he does not readily change his mind. If additional information or insight does become available the choleric may well change his decision but the change will be made just as quickly and confidently as the initial decision.

Cholerics are very strong-willed people and will argue forcefully to get their ideas accepted. In fact when others disagree with them they usually try to out-wit them in argument. The danger is that this sometimes leads to stubbornness where the choleric will stick to his decision just to prove a point. Perhaps it is too painful for them to admit that they have made a mistake. Attempts to make them change their minds, particularly where opinions, tastes and preferences are concerned, are almost always doomed to failure especially when they are confronted directly.

The Melancholy Partner

Melancholies do not find it easy to *express their affection* freely, even when they are strongly attracted to another. At first, Joy found it very difficult to express her love for me. She had been attracted to me for months before I even had an inkling about the way she felt.

Melancholies' moods are easily influenced by their emotions, and because they are inclined to be very introspective, much of their emotional energy is directed inwardly rather than outwardly towards their partners.

Melancholies are generally romantically-minded. They need the "right" kind of atmosphere to get into the mood for love. Low lights, soft music and intimate sharing all set the stage and enable them to express their affections. A melancholy husband complained to me that he hated it when his choleric wife wanted to make love on the spur of the moment. He felt that the atmosphere had to be right. The same man, however, did not very often tell his wife that he loved her, simply because he was too absorbed in his own emotions.

When it comes to *communicating,* melancholies seldom initiate the discussion, especially when it comes to sharing their innermost feelings. Melancholies tend to bottle things up, with an emotional outburst from time to time to relieve the pressure. Although melancholies do not often verbalise their emotions, they do communicate with the occasional sigh, the anguished expression, the silent withdrawal, which are all indications of their inner feelings.

Another aspect that hampers communication with a melancholy is the tendency to take things too personally. For example, when a husband describes what another woman has done to improve some aspect of her housekeeping, his melancholy wife may see this as a veiled criticism and immediately start defending herself. A friend of ours once told his wife that the problem with most women was that they take things too personally, to which his melancholy wife replied, "I don't."

Not only do melancholies take things too personally but they usually see things in a negative light. When friends have not been to visit us for some time, my melancholy wife will immediately say, "What's wrong with me? Have I done anything to offend them?" while I tend to say, "What's wrong with them?" Because of their touchiness their partners always have to be very careful of what to say and how to say it. The result is that the spontaneous flow of communication is severely restricted.

Most melancholies dislike having to *make decisions*. They are very indecisive by nature and their indecisiveness is of deep concern to them. It worries them that they can't make up their minds. When Joy and I go shopping together, conflict is sure to follow. She feels threatened by my quick decisions, while I am highly frustrated by her indecisiveness. Many a melancholy woman has bought a dress, changed it for another one and then, after having worn it once, decided that it didn't suit her after all and left it hanging in the wardrobe until the next jumble sale.

When melancholies encounter opposition to their ideas, they find it difficult to defend themselves with logical reasoning. They are usually beset with all kinds of emotions and usually tend to react emotionally. Walking off in a huff, or saying, "Just go ahead and do whatever you like," or sulking in the bedroom are all techniques that melancholies use to try to get their own way — often with great success, but it leaves their partners resentful and with a feeling of helplessness, because they have no resistance to such emotional behaviour.

The Phlegmatic Partner

Whereas melancholies find it difficult to *express their affection*, phlegmatics don't see any good reason for doing so regularly. Perhaps the most extreme case that I have come across is the wife who complained to her phlegmatic husband that he never told her that he loved her, to which he replied, "Cathy, 27 years ago I told you that I loved you. I also told you that if that ever changed, you would be the first to know."

Phlegmatics are generally very faithful marriage partners, and most of them expect their marriage partners to judge from their actions that they do love them. However, these actions are mostly those of fulfilling their role in marriage, like working hard to provide financial security or working hard to be a good household manager. The rare expression of love that is given spontaneously is often treasured by the partner. In a recent survey on what makes marriages happy, a number of wives related instances where their phlegmatic husbands had told them how much they cared for them. Partners of phlegmatics are usually starved of some spontaneous display of affection.

The phlegmatic's pattern of *communication* is characterised by the fact that he *does not*. By nature phlegmatics are very quiet — and what makes things worse is that it is very difficult to know what they are thinking. Unlike melancholies whose emotions are transparent, phlegmatics tend to remain stoic. They often give the impression of being rather critical though being too polite to mention it. Their lack of responsiveness and enthusiasm can drive a marriage partner up the wall, screaming for love and acceptance. On the other hand, phlegmatics don't become very emotional, and of all the temperaments they are probably the easiest to get along with. They make good listeners since they very seldom seek to propound their own ideas. They seldom become depressed and they can be a tower of strength and calm in a time of crisis.

When it comes to *decision-making*, phlegmatics are only too happy when other people make the decisions for them. Like melancholies, they too, are indecisive, but this doesn't bother them. Many of them postpone a decision in the hope that the problem will resolve itself. When pressed for a decision they often respond with, "Well, I haven't had much time to think about it."

Phlegmatic husbands tend to abdicate their position as leaders in the home, with the result that their wives are forced to take over that role, sometimes with serious consequences. For example, research has shown that a greater percentage of happy and well-adjusted children come from homes where the husband is clearly the head of the home, than from homes where he has abdicated this role.

Phlegmatics are usually happy to go along with the ideas of others. When a phlegmatic wife says, "That's fine, dear," she usually means it. However, problems arise when decisions that have to be made are left hanging in the air. This can become a great source of frustration and irritation to the marriage partner.

Why do opposites attract?

Opposite temperaments are not always attracted to each other. Couples with the same temperament do sometimes marry. If they are two phlegmatics it could mean a very *tranquil* relationship, but with many things left undone. If they are two melancholies, it would be a very *creative* partnership, but a very emotional relationship with many ups and downs. If they are two cholerics it is likely to be a very *stormy* relationship but also a very productive one in terms of accomplishments. If they are two sanguines it would probably be a virtual *non-stop talking match* but with a tremendous amount of fun into the bargain.

In the majority of marriages however, the partners have different temperaments. The reason for this is that we are often attracted to people who exhibit strengths that we do not have. A melancholy girl may be attracted to a choleric boy because he is so full of self-confidence. A phlegmatic boy may be attracted to a sanguine girl because she is always so lively and full of fun. The choleric man may be attracted to a phlegmatic woman because he finds her easy-going temperament so relaxing, or a sanguine woman may be attracted to a melancholy temperament because he is such an intellectual thinker.

Why so much conflict then?

The problem arises after the honeymoon is over and we discover that *our* strengths are *their* weaknesses. It is at this point that the couple has to make a crucial decision. Either they will focus more on each other's strengths than on their weaknesses, or they will concentrate on their weaknesses rather than on their strengths. If they focus on the weaknesses they will embark on a steady process of destruction. Each little criticism and each little fault pointed out will not lead to a change in the partner's behaviour, but it will increase their feelings of inferiority and is sure to evoke a counter-attack.

Recently a couple who had been married for more than 25 years told me the sad story of how they had been destroying each other through the years, till there was virtually nothing left of their relationship. Their personalities, too, had suffered. He had become a hard cynic, she a nervous wreck.

When our shortcomings are constantly pointed out, we usually respond in one of two ways
  — we either withdraw into a shell of inferiority, or
  — we become highly critical of our partners, breaking them down in the process — a vicious circle.

No one temperament would make a good marriage partner. Each temperament has some wonderful strengths — and some glaring weaknesses. Living with an extreme choleric who constantly dominates his mate could make a woman neurotic. Living with an extreme sanguine who is weak-willed and highly impulsive could drive a man round the bend. Living with an extreme phlegmatic who never takes any responsibility could well cause despair. An extreme melancholy who lives entirely by her emotions could cause endless frustration.

The answer does not lie in finding a partner with the right temperament — the answer lies in *learning to cope* with each other's temperaments.

Is there hope for us?

What's the use of trying?

At first we all try to resolve the conflicts that arise in our marriages — but as the incidences of conflict increase there comes a feeling of "what's the use?" The process of trying and failing, trying and failing, trying again and failing again may become so painful that we may stop trying. Then we can either withdraw physically by getting divorced — or mentally by living under the same roof in a meaningless relationship.

Divorce, however, is *not* the answer — all it amounts to is swopping one set of strengths and weaknesses for another set of strengths and weaknesses (if the second partner has a different temperament to the first one). Withdrawing mentally is not the answer either for it simply means that we stop developing as individuals.

No, the answer lies in learning to cope with our differences
— first of all by allowing God to take control of our lives and changing us
— secondly by responding differently to our partners.

Our reactions must change

The real problem is not the way our partners behave — it is the way we react to their behaviour. We can view the same behaviour either in a positive light or in a negative light. That is why we sometimes get irritated with our partner's behaviour although we used to admire it in our days of courtship. Similarly we can learn to react positively to behaviour we usually find most annoying.

As a choleric I often come up with new ideas — some of them rather controversial. This used to irritate Joy very much, and she often accused me of "always wanting to be different". This of course upset me. She has however, come to appreciate that this is all part of my initiative — and now admires me for my original thinking instead of criticising me for it. My behaviour is still the same, but her reactions are different.

As a melancholy she is inclined to foresee all the potential problems whenever I come up with a new project. This used to annoy me, and I accused her of "always being negative". However, I have realised that in my optimism I often tend to overlook the pitfalls and I have now come to really appreciate her critical analysis. Again, her behaviour hasn't changed but my reaction has — and a great deal of unnecessary conflict has been avoided.

In the rest of this chapter we will discuss five basic rules or approaches that will enable couples to cope with the temperament differences in their marriage relationship.

Acceptance

Probably the most important rule to follow is: *Don't try to change your partner.* Accept them as they are. So often we want our partners to react as *we* do — to see things the way we see them, to behave the way we do and even to think the way we do. That is a natural desire. However, the problem originates in the way we try to change them. Most of us hope to change our partners by pointing out the weaknesses and highlighting the shortcomings, but this kind of fault-finding not only fails to bring about a change but actually increases the partner's resistance to change.

Whenever an individual is criticised — even when the criticism is valid — he feels that he is being *attacked* and the natural reaction is to *defend*. The partner can defend himself in several ways. He can either counter-attack by highlighting the attacker's shortcomings, or he can withdraw and build an emotional shield around himself. For example, many a husband has developed a shield of total indifference to protect himself from his wife's persistent nagging and many a wife has withdrawn into her own little world — safe from her husband's constant fault-finding.

To add fuel to the fire, we so often attack the *person* rather than the *behaviour*. It's one thing to say, "Every time you correct me in company, I feel very foolish" — it's another thing to say, "You always want to make me look foolish in company." In the first case the behaviour is being attacked — in the second case the person is being attacked.

Accepting your partner as he is, therefore, does not mean putting up with all kinds of undesirable and unacceptable behaviour. It means letting your partner know what behaviour or attitude upsets you without making any attempt to change his or her behaviour. Leave the decision to change to them. Don't exert pressure of any kind. It won't change matters anyway.

Reinforcement

The most effective way to change your partner is to give him or her lots of praise and to express your appreciation as often as possible. *Build on their strengths.* Let them know what they are good at. Let them know what you like about them. Give them recognition for their efforts.

A business colleague whose marriage was virtually on the rocks admitted to me that whenever his wife did anything well, he said nothing — almost as if he expected it of her. But whenever she did anything wrong, or anything that he did not like, he was very quick to point it out to her. After listening to one of my talks he started making an effort to correct the situation by paying more attention to her and complimenting her more frequently. But he had a hard time at first. For example, when he complimented her on the nice shoes she was wearing, she said, "Thank you, but I've had them for over a year." He kept working at it, however, and today they are an extremely happy couple.

For some reason we are so quick to point out any negative aspect, while the positive one's are taken for granted. Another business colleague told me how his wife once blew her top when he refused dessert at supper one evening because he didn't particularly like it. She accused him of *never* liking the food she spent so much time in preparing. "You *always* criticise my cooking," she said, "you've always got something to say." "That's not true," he replied, "last night I said nothing!" I think that incident speaks volumes.

When last did you compliment your wife on her appearance, on the way she handles the children, on the way she runs the house? When last did you thank your husband for the way he provides for you, for his work around the house, for the security he provides? Don't take these things for granted.

Can one overdo it? Probably yes, but the likelihood of that is very slim, if the praise is
— genuine and sincere
— linked to actual achievement
— given freely without ulterior motives.

In other words avoid flattery or trying to manipulate your partner with smooth talk. There are enough good qualities that we *can* praise honestly.

Complementing

This means *supplementing your partner* in an area where he or she may be weak. Cholerics can be a tremendous help to their melancholy partners if they help to organise things — instead of criticising them for being so disorganised.

Phlegmatics can help their sanguine partners to think an issue over calmly — instead of ridiculing them for their impulsiveness. Melancholies can help their choleric partners by giving the children an extra dose of TLC (tender loving care) — instead of accusing them of unsympathetic behaviour towards the kids. Sanguines can take over some of the social obligations — instead of forcing their phlegmatic partners to be sociable.

For example, one husband looks after the two small children for one hour each day to allow his wife time to play the piano, and to continue with her music studies. In another home the wife handles all the financial administration, because she is more organised than her husband. (She does however, leave the financial decisions to him.)

Specific needs differ from couple to couple but the same principle holds good: *Where can we complement our partners so that they can concentrate on doing what they are best at?*

Feedback

Another means of helping us cope with each other's temperaments is to *provide helpful feedback* whenever we observe negative behaviour. In one family the couple agreed on an innocent statement like "the moon is round" whenever one partner saw the other behaving inappropriately. Whenever the wife, for instance, reacts too emotionally towards the children (she is a melancholy) the husband will say, "The moon is round," or if he reacts too harshly towards them (he is a choleric) she will do the same. In this way they help each other to prevent their weaknesses from dominating their behaviour.

The key to giving this kind of help, however, is a previous *agreement* between the husband and wife that they will do this — otherwise the help is seen as just another form of criticism with all the accompanying negative consequences.

Thanksgiving

The final step towards coping with your partner's temperament is to *thank God daily for your partner* as he or she is — with all the strengths and weaknesses. God knew what He was doing when he joined you two together — and by giving thanks to Him we express our faith and trust in Him in a very practical manner.

The amazing thing is that as we *act* in giving thanks, so we begin to acquire a thankful *attitude*. There is ample psychological evidence that behaviour affects our attitudes as much as attitudes affect our behaviour. When we begin to treat our partners differently, two things will happen

— they will start to behave according to the way we treat them
— we will start to see them in a new light, and behave towards them accordingly.

We therefore have the choice of either launching our relationship into an upward cycle — building on each other's strengths or launching our relationship into a downward spiral — breaking each other down.

Kneecap session

At this stage it would be a valuable experience for you and your partner to have a *kneecap session*.

Pick a time and place where you are not likely to be disturbed. Take two upright chairs and face one another so that your kneecaps touch. Then ask one another the following questions

1. Which temperament characteristics of mine cause friction and conflict in our relationship?
2. In which areas would you like me to accept you more?
3. In which way do I react inappropriately? In what way could I react differently?
4. What do you consider to be my strengths? What do I do particularly well? What do you particularly like about me?
5. In which areas can I give you more support? What can I do to complement you?
6. On what behaviour would you like me to give you feedback? How would you like me to give you that feedback?

Close your session with prayer — both thanking God for your partner as he or she is.

Some kneecap rules

1. Don't attack the *person* — only describe the *behaviour* that causes conflict.
2. Don't *defend* yourself. It's not important what your real motives were. The way your partner perceived your behaviour is the important issue.
3. If the discussion becomes too emotional — agree to *postpone* the discussion until you have both calmed down.
4. *Write* down your comments and agreements as far as possible — it makes the discussion more objective.

Part 3:
Joint decision-making

Watch your style

Who wants a robot?

Discussing some of his earlier courtships, a friend of ours told us that he had once dated a girl who expressed admiration for almost *everything* he said. Every time he expressed an opinion or shared a thought, she would say something like, "Wow! you're right! I never thought of it that way." Initially he found this rather flattering but, after several dates, it went sour. She didn't seem to have any opinions of her own and, as he phrased it, he "didn't want to be married to a robot".

Nobody wants to be married to partners who cannot think for themselves, who have no particular viewpoints, who seldom express their own opinions. Such a person may be suited to someone who feels personally threatened whenever anyone disagrees with him — but most of us want marriage partners who can stand on their own feet.

The problem is that once we've married them, these partners *do* stand on their own feet and they express their definite points of view. When these views differ from our own the scene is set for marital conflict.

The second dimension

During courtship the relationship is characterised by mainly one dimension — *communication*. People who are attracted to each other spend a good deal of time talking to each other and doing things together. This is how the relationship develops. When two people who were initially attracted to one another, find that they have very little in common, the relationship soon peters out. Communication is therefore essential for the development of any meaningful relationship.

It is this intimate communication that makes the courtship so thrilling — the wonder of discovering one another as individuals, the depth of emotion released when we share our innermost being with someone who cares and wants to listen. The enjoyment of just being together, of doing things together, is the theme of many love songs. This generates the "vibes", gives us goose-pimples, and sends that tingling sensation up our spine.

During courtship the entire focus of the relationship is on how we can please one another. But the moment we make a more permanent commitment, a second dimension enters the relationship — *joint decision-making.*

Up to now the individuals have been making their own decisions. They have been shopping to their own personal tastes, or going to places which stimulated their own personal interests. But marriage changes all that. They now discover that the tastes, desires and interests of their partners are equally important, and when these clash with their own, conflict is in the pipeline.

The potential for conflict

The adage that "love is blind, but marriage is an eye-opener" is all too true for most couples. Most couples believe that their love is so strong that it will smooth over all their differences — and when it doesn't, they begin to think that there is something wrong with their love.

Of course this is absurd. Whenever two people have to make decisions together, there will always be differences of opinion because each individual is different. Conflict in marriage is not bad or evil — it is a common ingredient in every marriage. When a couple tell their friends that they never have any differences of opinion, they are either being untruthful, or the spirit of one partner has been crushed by the other.

If not handled correctly, differences of opinion can and do create an *element of competitiveness.* For example, *she* may want a new lounge suite and *he* may think that the present suite is perfectly adequate. Various methods of persuasion will now be adopted by both partners — each trying to prove his own point. In the end one of them is going to win, and one of them is going to lose.

In the process there is a noticeable shift from seeking to please one another to *focussing on their own interests.* This is particularly evident when it comes to deciding on how to spend the money.

Obviously a situation like this will immediately reduce the level of intimate communication because the spouse may now be viewed as an opponent rather than as a partner in the true sense of the word. There may be a good deal of communication by way of reasoning and arguing, but this is not the kind of communication that strengthens a relationship.

The issue — how to handle conflict

The important issue is therefore not whether there is conflict in our marriage but how to handle the conflict we are confronted with. By conflict I do not mean a stand-up fight — although it could lead to that! By conflict I mean differences of opinion, and since differences will always crop up, we want to concentrate on how to deal with them. This is the cornerstone to building a successful marriage. A couple who have a happy relationship that brings out the best in both partners are a couple who have learned to handle their conflict successfully.

It is important to remember that handling conflict is only essential in an interdependent relationship. We may have great differences of opinion on a wide range of subjects with other acquaintances. However, these differences of opinion do not need to be resolved, since we do not have to make decisions together. Even good friends can have differences of opinion that do not necessarily affect their friendship. It is only the conflict that arises in the course of making decisions together in marriage that needs to be dealt with effectively.

Styles of handling conflict

Whenever we observe a husband and wife coping with conflict we can identify two aspects in the way they react to differences of opinion.

The first aspect is the *extent to which a person values his own ideas and interests*. We could mark a position on a scale from Low to High that would indicate the extent to which each person focusses on his own opinions and desires.

The second aspect is the *extent to which a person values the ideas of his partner*. Again we could mark a position on a scale ranging from Low to High, showing the extent to which he focusses on his partner's opinions and desires.

When we bring these two scales together we can identify five distinct approaches to conflict-handling — as shown in the diagram below

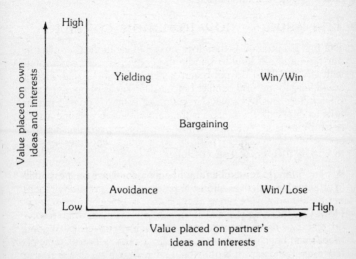

The avoidance style

People who follow this approach to conflict-handling do not value their own interests very highly, nor those of their partners. They very seldom express any opinions or desires on the assumption that if they don't say anything, nobody can disagree with them, thereby avoiding any conflict.

They will avoid committing themselves as far as possible, preferring to leave the decisions to their partners. Some become very good at talking without saying anything. This may range from making grunting noises behind a newspaper, to saying, "That's worth thinking about" — but they will never broach the subject again themselves.

Some give the impression of wanting peace at all costs. They often exhibit a "couldn't be bothered" attitude, and in essence tell their partners that "Whatever you decide is okay by me." Such marriage partners are mentally and emotionally divorced, even though they are still together physically.

When this approach to handling conflict is followed it usually leads to the other partner's taking over the decision-making role — and with time they begin to exclude their partners from the decision-making process. They no longer bother to consult them or take their partners' interests into consideration — which in turn leads to greater avoidance and withdrawal.

Avoiding conflict is a poor way of dealing with it. On the surface it may achieve domestic peace and lack of conflict but it will eventually destroy the relationship. At first the avoiding partner will go along with his mate's decisions — albeit without enthusiasm. In time this lack of enthusiasm will be followed by resentment and bitterness.

This style of handling conflict is unnatural. It is a forced style which develops most frequently in response to a domineering partner who tackles conflict in a win/lose manner. Withdrawing and avoiding such conflict then becomes a defence mechanism against the pain of losing the argument.

The yielding style

This style of handling conflict is adopted by people who do not place a high value on their own ideas and interests but who value the ideas and interests of their partners very highly.

Although they do have their own opinions and desires they are quite willing to change them or set them aside for the sake of their partners. This can stem either from a very high regard for their partners and a low regard for themselves. or from a desire to please their partners at all costs.

People who crave affection and approval and who find security in "just being together" will gladly accept their partner's views and decisions. Their whole attitude is one of "As long as you're happy, Honey, I don't mind." Sometimes this approach is seen as the Christian virtue of "being willing to be the least". There is certainly nothing wrong with putting your partner's interests before your own — but when this becomes the pattern whenever differences of opinion arise, it will have a harmful effect on the marriage relationship.

In the first place it may mean that a valuable contribution to the decision may be lost. It is well known for example that a strong opposition party will always keep a democratically-elected government on its toes — and ensure better decisions. Similarly a wife may have excellent insight into a problem but, if she does not express this seriously because she feels she has to support her husband whole-heartedly, he may in fact make a less effective decision.

An even more serious consequence to the marriage is the loss of respect for the yielding partner. The girl referred to at the beginning of this chapter, who expressed admiration for whatever her companion said, is a good example of this type of handling conflict. With time she would stop resolving any serious issues for herself and become completely dependent upon her partner's views. She would in fact become a mental robot.

There is a real danger that this style of handling conflict may become confused with the biblical concept of submission. Many wives who want to obey God's principle of submission end up as doormats by giving in every time a difference of opinion arises. Some even lose their own identity in the process and this does not lead to a strong marriage, nor does it illustrate the principle of submission.

The bargaining style

This approach to handling conflict is sometimes described as "meeting each other halfway". People who follow this approach to handling conflict value their partner's interests as much as their own. Their basic premise however, is that their differences cannot be reconciled and must therefore be traded off against each other. There is neither a yielding, nor an attempt to change their partner's views — only an attempt to arrive at some sort of compromise, through a process of bargaining.

This *may* mean meeting each other halfway. He may want to spend a two-week holiday at the seaside, while she may want to spend the holiday at her mother's. A compromise may be reached by agreeing to spend one week at each place.

A far more common approach, however, is to trade desires. She may agree to spend the two weeks at the seaside *on condition* that he agrees to spend the following Christmas vacation at her parents' home. He will agree to buy her a new lounge suite, *if* she lets him play golf every Saturday. Each time it is a conditional agreement, as in a commercial transaction.

The worst kind of bargaining is where the wife uses sexual inter-course as a trading commodity. She agrees to make love *if* he agrees to help her with the dishes that evening. There won't be much love in such love-making. However, there are times when a compromise is the only way to resolve the conflict. When the interests and viewpoints are so drastically opposed that no common ground can be found, a compromise may be the best solution after all.

On the other hand when bargaining becomes the typical way of handling conflict it can be very detrimental to the marriage rela-tionship. The husband or wife may begin to store up incidents to use as bargaining points. For example, when the husband buys a new fishing rod, the wife who uses this style of handling conflict may say to herself, "I'll remember that when I want money for a new coat." Or if she invites her mother to spend a week or two with them even though her husband doesn't get on very well with his mother-in-law, he may keep this in reserve "for the next time".

Each partner begins to look after his or her own interests. They begin to "keep score" and with time the love that once motivated them to give freely to each other, begins to fade. Nevertheless this approach is less harmful than the yielding or the avoidance ap-proach, even though it does lead to a mediocre relationship.

The win/lose style

This is probably the most common approach to handling conflict in marriage. Here a person places a very high value on his own opinions and desires and very little on those of his partner. Peo-ple who use this style of handling conflict are usually very con-cerned that things should happen the way *they* want them to hap-pen, and they will go to great lengths to ensure this. In other words they look upon conflict as a contest that must be *won* and they usually approach it in such a way that their partners must lose.

People use a variety of techniques to get their own way, and these techniques will be described in greater detail in the next sec-tion.

What effect does the win/lose style have on the marriage rela-tionship? Basically there are three possible outcomes. The first is where husband and wife are constantly at each other, each trying his utmost to win. Some couples seem to thrive on this, and we can refer to them as the "happy warriors". However, their relationship becomes a battle of wits — the one trying to outwit the other — and in the process the relationship comes to a standstill. There is no growing together, no personal development, no intimate communication. In such circumstances it would be far too risky to share any weaknesses or fears, since these might well be used as ammunition against oneself in the next round. And without intimate communication a relationship cannot grow and blossom.

A second possibility is that one partner constantly "wins" against his or her mate. The losing partner will eventually begin to withdraw from the relationship in order to avoid the conflict — and the relationship deteriorates. The avoidance approach is the best line of defence for those who cannot win against their partners.

The third possible effect is the withdrawal of both partners. These are the "weary wranglers", whose arguments fizzle out to an unresolved stalemate. The pain of arguing endlessly becomes so vivid that both begin to avoid controversial issues, and in the process they begin to drift apart. The conflict remains unresolved while the relationship slowly disintegrates.

The win/win style

This is the approach where full value is placed on both partners' interests, views and desires. Neither partner gives in, neither partner seeks to win. The question is always *"What is right?"* Both partners strive for consensus, that is, both agree fully (or at least partially) on the particular course of action to be taken. The conflict is resolved in such a manner that both partners feel satisfied and their relationship is strengthened.

It is only when couples learn to handle conflict in this manner, that the relationship becomes an enriching one. It is only in this kind of relationship that they can find marital happiness — where each individual can grow and develop as a person.

Later we will discuss in greater detail what this win/win approach entails and how couples can develop this style in their own marriage relationship.

If you win ... you lose

Foul fighting

What is the function of a referee in a boxing match? Certainly not to stop the fighting. In fact when there's a boxing match, two people will always be fighting. No, the referee is there to make sure that there is no *foul* fighting. It is quite alright for two people to fight, as long as they adhere to the rules of fair fighting.

What a pity that there is no referee to monitor our marital conflicts. For the problem is not the fighting itself, but our particular style of fighting. Unfortunately it would seem that in most of our marital conflicts, foul fighting is the rule rather than the exception — and the injured partner has no one to appeal to when a foul blow is delivered.

When one or both partners adopt a win/lose approach to handling conflict they are out to win — and "winning" to them means "getting their own way". There are basically two ways in which to get your own way. One is *direct attack*, the other is *subtle manipulation*. As we mature, each one of us learns which techniques are the most effective. A little girl may find that when she stages a big performance in the supermarket she is very likely to get some sweets if she screams loudly enough, since Mum will do anything to avoid embarrassment. When that same little girl becomes a little wife, she may continue to kick up a big fuss in order to get her own way, the only difference being that by now she has learned to refine the technique *and* to use it very effectively.

We'll discuss *five attacking techniques* first, viz. reasoning, kitbagging, blaming, criticising and ridiculing. Then we'll look at *five manipulating techniques*, viz. smooth-talking, claiming helplessness, suffering, withdrawing and self-deprecation. Although there are many variations, most foul fighting can be classified under one of these techniques.

Reasoning

In most marriages one partner is usually able to think more quickly than the other partner. People who can formulate their thoughts rapidly are usually able to verbalise them effortlessly, and this gives them a decided advantage when engaged in an argument with their partners.

Some time ago Joy and I were discussing a particular course of action that she should take. Because I can verbalise my thoughts quickly, I immediately suggested a course of action, and listed three reasons, one ... two ... and three ... She responded with, "Yes, I suppose you are right", and followed my suggestion. Several hours later she came home in a fury. "I'm not going to listen to you again! I won't allow myself to be dominated! I should have followed my own ideas!" She then proceeded to tell me why my suggestion was off the mark, and gave some excellent reasons why her idea was by far the better one. I was quite taken aback and asked her why she hadn't mentioned these reasons at the time. "Because when you come up with point one ... point two ... point three ... I can't think anymore!" she replied.

By my quick reasoning, I had "won" the argument, because Joy had not been able to provide a good counter-argument. But both of us had "lost" — and our relationship had suffered. We have since learned that simply because Joy cannot provide an immediate counter-argument, does not mean that there isn't one. As a result I now help her to formulate *her* thoughts, before expressing my own point of view.

There is nothing wrong with logical, sound reasoning, unless presented in an overpowering manner or with the intention of out-arguing your partner in order to "win", which reflects a win/lose approach. One partner may win, but if in the process the other partner loses, then both have lost, because the relationship is affected negatively.

Kitbagging

Here one partner has an imaginary kitbag. Every little injury, every little offence, every little hurt is carefully stored in the kitbag. At the time nothing much is said. The person who uses this technique usually suffers in silence — until the kitbag is full. Then when the next disagreement occurs (and usually it's an insignificant issue) there is an explosion! All the pent-up feelings and emotions come pouring out — usually to the utter amazement and total disbelief of the other partner, who simply cannot understand why such a small issue should bring about such an intense reaction. As one friend explained to me, "When my wife and I have an argument she usually becomes historical." "You mean hysterical," I replied. "No, historical. She keeps bringing up the past."

Few people can withstand such a barrage of emotions, and most of us would succumb to such an onslaught. The people who use this technique therefore get their own way, and they start storing up "ammunition" again until there is enough in the kitbag to warrant another outburst.

Again, one of the partners may win, but the relationship suffers, and with time the other partner will become immune to these emotional outbursts. The outbursts will have to increase in volume and intensity, if they are to have the desired effect.

Blaming

A useful technique to get your own way is to blame your partner for the things that go wrong. If your partner points out any faults in your behaviour, you can always get him off your back by blaming him for it and making him feel guilty.

A friend of ours had often asked his wife to have supper ready at 17h30 so that he could have more time available in the evening. Whenever she was late with supper she didn't wait for him to criticise her — she delivered the first blow by telling him that he expected too much of her and that he made impossible demands on her. By doing this she made sure that she "won" before the conflict over the late supper had even surfaced — but it did nothing to enhance the atmosphere in the home.

It is easy to blame your partner and to arouse his feelings of guilt. "You make me angry. You never help me around the house. You never take an interest in my work. If it wasn't for you, I would have been able to .... " etc. This seldom accomplishes anything, for attack leads to counter-attack and both partners end up on the losing side.

Criticism

Closely linked to blaming, is fault-finding. This is very easy to do for we are all aware of our partner's shortcomings. A wife may complain to her husband about his trampling mud into her clean lounge carpet. He immediately counters with an attack on her appearance — that she's always walking around in curlers. This may put her on the defensive, so that he "wins" the argument about the dirty carpets. But he forgets about the resentment she harbours as a result of his criticism.

When we criticise our partners, we often tend to generalise. "You *never* hang up your clothes." "You *always* come home late." Such generalisations are seldom true. It's a foul way of fighting — and nobody ever wins.

Whenever people are dissatisfied with themselves they tend to find fault with others — particularly those closest to them. Because they cannot cover up their shortcomings in front of their partners they feel vulnerable and exposed. They try to counteract their feelings of inferiority by constantly criticising their partners and at the same time keep their partners at bay. No relationship can survive in such conditions. Husband and wife become entangled in a vicious circle of attack and counter-attack. In the process they destroy each other. No wonder that God warns us that if we "keep on biting and devouring each other" we will destroy each other (Galatians 5:15).

Ridiculing

All the techniques described so far, with the exception of reasoning, have concentrated on getting your own way by attacking your partner *as a person*. In most cases it is not the problem that is attacked, or the inappropriate behaviour — but the individual himself, or some personal characteristic. This is particularly evident when a person resorts to ridiculing as a method of getting his own way.

Ever heard a husband tell his wife not to be so stupid? Or a wife saying to her husband, "What do you know about a thing like this?" I have sometimes used high-flown words, and when my wife asked the meaning I have replied, "What! don't you know what it means?" in such a deprecating manner that she stopped asking. It was one way to win an argument, but it was definitely not a healthy one.

One of the most common ways of ridiculing is to accuse your partner of being childish. Another way is to laugh condescendingly in response to an opinion expressed by your partner, with a "how-naive-can-you-get"-look.

These techniques are all aimed at demolishing the opposition. They may be acceptable practices in parliament (although even there they can be very counter-productive) but in marriage they are devastating. The relationship always loses — and subsequently both husband and wife lose, regardless of who "wins" the argument.

By all means, let's "fight" — conflict is a natural part of marriage. But let's keep it clean and fair. Foul fighting leads to both parties being disqualified — both lose as far as personal growth is concerned.

Smooth-talking

All of the above techniques represent the direct-attack approach to getting one's own way. There are however, more subtle forms of manipulation that can be extremely effective. One of them is a smooth tongue. Probably the most common form is open flattery. A man invites some friends home for dinner and only tells his wife about it when they arrive at the front door. There in front of all his friends she hears from him — for the first time — what a marvelous cook she is and how amazingly quickly she can prepare a meal. Or a wife may come to her husband and tell him how wonderful he is, how generous he has always been, how she appreciates the fact that she always feels at liberty to ask him for extra money — and then ask him for a new dress. This is undisguised manipulation.

We all enjoy compliments, but when they are given with an ulterior motive, they leave a bitter taste in the mouth. That is why a man who very seldom compliments his wife and then all of a sudden starts praising her, is likely to get only one response: "What do you want from me?" One cannot blame her for being suspicious.

Another approach to getting our own way is to placate our partners when they express reservations about our plans. "Don't worry about it, Sweetheart. You'll see that it will all turn out well. Trust me." This is just another way to overcome any opposition. It is not good partnership.

Claiming helplessness

It is much easier to give an explanation for our behaviour

than to change it. Somehow we believe that if we can come up with a good enough excuse, we can justify almost any behaviour. Traditional psychiatry has done us a great disservice by suggesting that there are behavioural forces over which we have no control. A man may for example suggest to his wife that she should express her affection for him more openly. If she replies, "What can you expect when I had a mother who never expressed her affection openly?" she is claiming helplessness in order to get her own way.

There are probably as many excuses as there are people. Some blame their backgrounds, while others use illness to get their own way. "How can you expect me to do this, when you know I'm so ill?" Some people even use God to get their own way. Men have neglected their families — even financially, with the excuse that God had told them to do this or that. Women have been "conned" into marriage because their prospective husbands have claimed that God had shown them to be their life partners. That's a get-my-own-way technique if ever there was one!

People who use this manipulative approach are basically claiming to be helpless — that they are subject to circumstances and forces over which they have no control. Since it becomes almost impossible to counter such reasoning effectively, people who resort to this technique usually end up winning — or at least getting their own way, but again with serious negative consequences for the relationship.

Suffering

A third manipulative technique is to let our partners know how much suffering they are causing us. One of the most common ways is to let our partners know that they have hurt our feelings. Since they then become responsible for our hurt feelings, the obligation is on them to change their behaviour — and we've "won" again.

In a marriage where love-making was not very frequent, the wife used to blame the husband by saying, "You make me feel so awful when you ask me to make love and I'm not up to it. I just feel I'm a complete failure as a woman." What she really wanted of course was for him to stop asking, and when he did "because I

65

didn't want to make my wife feel a failure", she had succeeded in getting her own way.

A husband who occasionally has a drink with his colleagues after work can be manipulated to come home on time every evening, because his wife worries so much when he stays out late. It actually brings on severe headaches, and what self-respecting man would wilfully cause his wife to suffer from headaches?

Tears can also be used effectively to get one's own way — as many women know so well. Very few men can cope with a tearful wife, especially if she also accuses him of "not loving her anymore". Rather than say to her, "You are obviously very upset right now. Let's continue the discussion when you've had a chance to calm down," the husband allows himself to feel guilty for causing his wife "so much anguish". Subsequently he gives in in order to pacify her — and she has won. In fact any woman who starts off a proposition by saying, "If you really loved me, you would …" is simply manipulating her husband to get her own way.

Another tactic often used is to walk away from an argument with a "do whatever you like, I couldn't care less" remark. People who say this do not really mean it. They really do care what happens. It is just another get-my-own-way technique. What woman will freely go ahead and "do whatever she likes" after her husband has told her to do just that?

Perhaps the most extreme form of suffering used to manipulate someone's behaviour is to threaten suicide. A young woman told me the story of how her father had committed suicide and that as a young teenager she somehow felt that she was to blame. When some years later her boyfriend threatened to kill himself if she didn't go to bed with him, she couldn't bear the thought of being responsible for another death. So she finally gave in — and ended up with an illegitimate child.

Some marriages have been founded on the threat of suicide. A middle-aged man told us of his unhappy marriage of over twenty years. When he had wanted to break off the engagement, his fiancée had threatened to commit suicide — so he had married her. Hardly a prescription for a happy relationship. He felt trapped and the subsequent bitterness virtually destroyed both him and his wife.

Withdrawing

A particularly foul method of fighting is to say nothing, to withdraw in silence. This is a very loud silence that permeates every aspect of home life. It is not unusual for me as counsellor to hear of husbands who don't talk to their wives for days on end. When their partners beg them to tell them what the matter is, the only answer they get is a stoic "nothing". Every now and then I hear of wives who walk around the house with martyred expressions but who refuse to express their grievances. Their husbands are expected to guess what the trouble is.

This is a very immature approach to handling conflict. Underlying this technique is a basic desire on the part of some individuals to punish their partners because they couldn't get their own way. They want to punish them for some real or imagined injury, or because things didn't turn out the way they wanted them to.

For the partner on the receiving end of this treatment, it *is* a punishment. Not knowing what one has said or done to cause offence can be nerve-racking. The result is that one either humbles oneself by asking forgiveness "for anything I *may* have done to upset you" or one withdraws as well. In this case the atmosphere in the house will become "formally polite" — that of two people merely sharing the same roof.

If this approach to handling conflict becomes the pattern, the marriage relationship can only go one way — downhill. Eventually the partner on the receiving end may withdraw physically. This was the case with a young couple who had been married for less than three years. The husband simply refused to talk to his wife for days on end, until she could stand it no longer and went back to her mother — 600 km away.

Individuals who use this style of handling conflict usually pretend to be the offended party. They are the ones who have been hurt, and are "deeply grieved" — or so it would seem. In most cases, however, they are upset because they couldn't get their own way and they resort to silence as a means of "getting even". As with the other get-my-own-way techniques, nobody really wins, and both partners lose in the end.

Self-deprecation

Probably the most unfair method of fighting is to run yourself down, to feel sorry for yourself, to tell your partner what a failure you are or how hopeless you are.

I know of a woman who uses this approach to avoid having to accept responsibility for her own behaviour. "Don't worry, when I'm gone you can find yourself the perfect wife" is a typical comment, or she'll say something like, "What's the use of trying — nothing I do is ever good enough for you." Of course she doesn't *really* mean it — it's just a way of arousing her husband's sympathy, and it conveniently shifts the attention away from the problem.

Saying you're sorry can be intended as a genuine apology, but it can also be used as a method of warding off any criticism. A man may come home and apologise profusely to his wife. "I feel so terrible that I've let you and the kids down again. I was determined not to gamble again, but the boys at the office dragged me down to the racecourse and I'm afraid there isn't much left of my pay packet. Can you *ever* forgive me? Why don't you just leave me? You don't deserve to be married to a rotter like me." His wife would find it very hard to scold him — and so he gets away with it once more.

People who run themselves down seldom really mean it. They have learned that this approach usually evokes sympathy, but if their partners were to say to them, "I'm glad you've realised this. Why don't we discuss some plan of action to help you overcome this problem?" the response might be very awkward — because they would have to face the responsibility for their behaviour fairly and squarely.

Winning means losing

By now it must be pretty obvious that when we "win" against our partners, when we wangle things the way we want to — regardless of our partner's wishes — when we succeed in getting our own way, brushing aside all opposition, the victory is somehow not as sweet as we'd hoped for. There may be temporary satisfaction in winning an argument or outwitting our partners, but the relationship suffers as a result and both partners lose out.

A marriage relationship will either develop our potential as mature individuals or it will break us down. Very seldom does such a relationship leave the individual untouched. Nobody comes through a divorce unscathed. The sense of failure, the emotional pain and the loss of direction leave permanent scars no matter how hard we try to disguise them. This is true not only of a physical divorce but also of an emotional divorce. Two people who live together without experiencing a meaningful relationship will only destroy each other as individuals.

Divorce is certainly not the answer, for the next relationship will bring its own conflict, even though the reasons for it may differ. The only solution is to learn how to resolve marital conflict in a win/win manner.

It all depends on how you look at it

The role of emotions

Before we deal with the win/win approach I would like to look at the whole area of emotions and feelings, especially since the get-my-own-way techniques described in the previous section rely heavily on the rôle of emotions.

Emotions can be used as weapons to get one's own way. Many of the direct-attack techniques use the expression of anger as a weapon — and it can be a devastating weapon. Manipulative techniques also rely on emotions — on the willingness of our partners to accept responsibility for *our* emotions. A husband doesn't want to cause his wife anxiety, a wife feels responsible for her husband's silence, a woman doesn't want to feel responsible for her fiancé's suicide. If they were to refuse responsibility for their partners' emotions this technique would fail miserably.

Emotions, more than any other factor, can harm a relationship to such an extent that calm discussion, logical reasoning and objective analysis become almost impossible. The more two marriage partners are governed by their emotions, the more difficulty they will have in resolving their conflict successfully.

What causes emotional reactions?

Do we have any control over our emotions? Can we avoid losing our tempers? Can we prevent bouts of depression? Do we have any control over jealousy? Most people would probably answer "no", and be very quick to prove it. A little while ago, a friend of mine reacted very strongly to the idea that when we become angry we actually choose to become angry and he told me of an incident where he had offered to help an elderly man with a task but was promptly rebuffed: "Do you think that after all these years, I don't know my job?" My friend said he felt the blood rushing to his head, and only by exercising the utmost self-control did he refrain from losing his temper. But he *was* furious.

He told this story to illustrate that the anger had welled up involuntarily — that it had been an automatic reaction over which he had had no control. But was this so?

Many people believe that events *cause* emotional reactions. They believe that a sad story usually *makes* a person cry, that an insult invariably *makes* us angry and that a joke is bound to *make* us laugh.

However, not *all* people respond to the *same* situation in the *same* way. A specific incident will cause one person to become intensely annoyed, while another person will laugh it off. Two widows worked with me in the same office. Both were middle-aged and both had lost their husbands several years previously. The one was a cheerful soul, loved by everyone. The other was a bitter woman, who always reminded others of what "she had suffered because of her husband's death". Most of her colleagues avoided her as far as possible. These two people had experienced a similar tragedy — but their reactions were poles apart.

Nor does the same person always react in the same way to the same situation. An incident that will infuriate you one day may perhaps annoy you mildly the next. A story that brings tears to your eyes one day, may leave you unmoved the next.

It is therefore not the *event* that causes the emotional reaction, but the way you *think* about that event. The chap in the earlier example became furious because he thought that his kind offer of help had been rudely rejected. However, the old man who had rejected the offer may have seen it as a veiled hint that he was incompetent. That's why *he* reacted the way he did. If our friend had viewed the situation differently instead of becoming angry, he might have felt sympathy for an old man who had probably never received any recognition for his capabilities — it all depends on how you look at it.

Thoughts that cause problems

A young trainee manager complained bitterly about his immediate boss, because he was being given far too much responsibility. He thought that his boss was simply "passing the buck" and he obviously felt resentful. When pointed out to him that this was actually an indication of the high regard that his boss had for his capability, his whole attitude changed from resentment to pride, simply because he saw the situation in a new light.

Discussing what would probably happen if one partner had to die, a husband told his wife that he would probably get married again as soon as possible. She immediately thought, "He can't wait to get rid of me and marry some young popsy." Naturally she was very upset. But I have told Joy the same thing and her reaction was completely different, because to her it meant that I was enjoying my marriage and would probably want to marry someone just like her. She felt flattered.

Two students reacted completely differently to being turned down for a date. One student thought he was unattractive to girls, and just no good. He became very depressed when a girl refused a date. The other student thought, "What a pity for her she's not going to have the pleasure of my company." He then optimistically approached another girl for a date.

In both cases two people reacted completely differently to a situation because they viewed it, or thought about it, differently.

So often we tell ourselves that we *ought* to feel hurt or upset when something happens. If you spill your drink on somebody's dress, you can think "it's stupid of me to make such a mistake" and feel embarrassed, or you can think "we all have accidents like this once in a while", offer to have it cleaned and forget about it. When we analyse our thoughts about situations like these we find that many of them are irrational. A newly-wed man may be very upset after a disagreement with his wife. He may think "people who are in love shouldn't have disagreements", and so he feels depressed. That is however, not rational thinking — and as we have seen, not realistic either. Yet it is this line of thought which causes his depression, which will affect his relationship with his wife in a negative manner, and lead to further conflict.

Some of the most intense arguments between husband and wife originate as a result of a misunderstanding caused by irrational thoughts.

Can we change our reactions?

Yes, we *can* change the way we look at situations. We *can* change our thoughts about the things that happen to us and the things that people say to us. Irrational thoughts can be countered. When you think that you *should* feel bad because you arrived late for a meeting, you can counter it with something like, "My coming late was due to heavy traffic. It happens in the best of families." When you think that your partner doesn't love you anymore because he or she hasn't said so for a long time you can counter it

72

with, "Telling me isn't the only way to express love."

You may think, "I should feel embarrassed because my mother-in-law was rude to my friends," but if you say to yourself that "being embarrassed won't change anything except to make me feel bad — anyway I'm not responsible for my mother-in-law's actions" you may avoid a good deal of negative emotion.

Counter-thoughts from God's Word

The more we believe in a counter-thought, the quicker we will eliminate the irrational thoughts. That is why counter-thoughts that are based on God's truth are the most effective ones. Let's look at some irrational thoughts that we experience frequently and see how God counters them. And remember, when God gives a command He always provides the ability to obey Him.

- *"I couldn't help myself. Something just made me do it."* God says that each person will be held accountable for his own actions (Romans 14:12).
- *"Making that mistake was terrible. I'll never be able to forget it."* God says we are to forget the things that are behind us and focus on the future (Philippians 3:14).
- *"It is terrible when things go wrong."* God says that in all things He works for the good of those who love Him (Romans 8:28), therefore we are to thank Him for everything (Ephesians 5:20).
- *"I can't control my emotions."* God says His children must simply put away all anger, passion and hateful feelings (Colossians 3:8).
- *"I'm so worried about that situation."* God says we must cast our anxieties on Him because He cares for us (I Peter 5:7).
- *"I can't stand the way others act."* God says we are to be tolerant and forgiving towards others (Ephesians 4:32).
- *"If others criticise me, I must be at fault."* God says His disciples are to be glad when others slander them falsely (Matthew 5:11).
- *"I must never show my weakness."* God says that His strength is only revealed when we are weak (II Corinthians 12:9).
- *"I am inferior — just a nobody."* God says that those who belong to Him are a chosen people and a royal priesthood (I Peter 2:9).

73

The choice is ours

It is probably not accurate to say that when we become angry it's because we decide to be angry, or that when we are depressed it's because we choose to be depressed. However it is accurate to state that we can choose how to view a situation, how to think about it, how to interpret it. And remember, *how* we look at it determines our emotional reactions to it. We can either believe God, or believe our own feelings. The choice is ours!

Both of us can win

The win/win style

The win/win approach to handling conflict means that both partners place an equally high value on their own as well as their partner's views and desires. If these opinions and wishes clash when it comes to making decisions, these differences are negotiated in such a way that neither partner has to win, give in, bargain or run away. Trying to win would mean a win/lose approach. Giving in would reflect a yielding style. Bargaining would mean a compromise. Running away would mean avoiding the issue. Win/win means that the conflict is resolved in such a way that both partners win, and the relationship is strengthened.

Declare your wishes

Marriage partners can hold widely differing opinions without necessarily experiencing conflict. A woman may think that a particular movie star is wonderful. Her husband may disagree completely — yet it would not create conflict because it wouldn't affect any decisions that they would have to make. However, when differences *do* affect a decision in the home, the conflict has to be handled effectively.

Decisions always lead to some sort of outcome, some sort of action. Therefore, it is important right from the start, that each partner states specifically what he or she would like to happen. When a wife accuses her husband of not being demonstrative, she is not expressing a specific desire in terms of action. If however, she says, "I would like you to give me a hug at least once a day," she is declaring a specific wish in terms of what she would like the outcome to be.

These wishes must always be stated in the first person singular (so-called "I" messages) and they must always be expressed in terms of action or outcome rather than feelings. They must also be expressed without putting the partner under any kind of pressure. When a husband says to his wife, "You are more interested in your garden than in getting my supper ready on time," he is not using an "I" message and at the same time he is "accusing" her of neglecting her marital responsibility. It would be far easier to adopt the win/win approach: "I would like to eat my supper at 17h30 if possible." In this way he is not putting subtle pressure on her.

Other examples of "I" messages with reference to some of the cases mentioned previously might resemble the following

"I would like to spend our holiday at the seaside."

"I would like to buy a new car, rather than a new lounge suite."

"I would like to serve supper between 18h00 and 18h30."

"I would like you to give me more housekeeping money."

"I would like to have at least four hours notice of any dinner guests."

"I would like you to stop asking me to make love *every* evening."

These are wishes that leave no doubt about your partner's feelings *without* you having to exert any pressure on your partner.

Resolve the differences

When both partners have expressed their desires explicitly in terms of outcome, the stage is set for the discussion of any differences. To ensure a win/win approach during this phase, the couple must stick rigidly to the "*we versus it*" approach, as opposed to the "*you versus me*" approach. The "we versus it" approach implies that they are both on the same side, confronting a problem. The "you versus me" approach implies that they are on opposite sides confronting each other. When a wife tells her husband, "You never help me around the house," she is taking a "you versus me" approach in that she is directly confronting him. If she says, "I would appreciate your help around the house, because I can't cope with all the chores. Can we talk about it?" she is taking a "we versus it" approach. Notice the accusation in the "you versus me" statement and the positive approach in the "we versus it" statement.

There may still be times when your partner interprets this as an attack and comes up with all kinds of excuses to defend himself. The golden rule is *not* to join the argument or try to prove your point. Rather acknowledge the excuses and then go back to the problem. You might say, "Yes, I understand why you acted the way you did. But how do you think we can solve this problem?" In this way you avoid attacking the person (you versus me) and concentrate on attacking the problem (we versus it).

76

Let's illustrate this with an example in an area that is a common source of conflict — the amount of money that the wife spends on clothes. The win/lose approach is for the husband to accuse her of squandering his hard-earned money. This will immediately put the wife on the defensive and she'll come up with countless arguments to prove that she is not spending money unwisely — or she may counter-attack by accusing him of spending too much on motorcar accessories. In an argument like this nobody wins. Adopting the win/win approach the husband would probably start off by saying, "I would like you to balance your budget." In turn the wife would state her desire: "I would like you to give me a larger housekeeping allowance because I cannot make ends meet." Neither one has attacked the other, nor have they defended their actions. At this point they are ready to say, "How are we going to solve this problem?" and the stage is set for resolving the differences.

Resolving differences involves three basic steps
- obtaining relevant data
- listing all possible alternatives
- evaluating the alternatives.

Obtain relevant data

Relevant data means both factual information as well as reasons and insights. In our previous example the applicable factual information could be a record of housekeeping expenditure over the past few months, the increase in the price index of food and clothing, the level of income, how it is currently spent, etc. In discussing reasons and insights partners might compare the wife's present wardrobe with the estimated clothing needs for the season. She might point out her need for additional winter clothing, or remind him that her coat is twelve years old. He might point out that a present increase in allowance would mean a reduction in saving for the deposit on a house of their own.

When a couple adheres strictly to this approach, it somehow reduces the emotional content of the discussion. Data is impersonal and enables them both to view the situation more objectively, especially when the facts are written down.

One of the most severe arguments that Joy and I have ever had, lasted throughout the Friday evening and continued on the Saturday morning. By mid-morning we were simply hurling insults at each other — and the atmosphere was very tense. Just before lunchtime Joy suggested that we write down our differences. To our utter amazement (and relief) we discovered that there *were* no major differences. The worst fight of our marriage was due to a misunderstanding. The problem was that we had allowed our emotions to cloud the issue. We had stopped listening to each other, and had been trapped in a vicious attack/counter-attack cycle. By writing down the facts we were able to look at the situation objectively.

List the alternatives

It is very easy to get so involved in the discussion of one particular course of action, that we lose sight of other alternatives that are open to us. One couple was experiencing serious in-law problems. His mother used every possible opportunity to find fault with his wife and to run her down with the result that she lost all her self-confidence. One can imagine the tension this brought into their relationship. However, one evening this couple sat down and declared their wishes, wrote down all the relevant information and then listed about fourteen alternative ways of resolving the situation, providing a most valuable total perspective. Instead of arguing in circles they were able to focus their attention on a limited number of positive solutions.

In our example of the housekeeping allowance the alternatives listed might include stopping all clothes purchases for six months, reducing actual spending by 20% over the next year, increasing the allowance (with subsequent reduction elsewhere), drawing up a housekeeping budget, selling all outdated clothes, making a point of attending special sales offers, etc. etc.

While these alternatives are being listed they may *not* be discussed or even commented on. Remarks like "that will be the day", or "it will never work", must be avoided altogether. This is just a time of devising alternatives, no matter how inappropriate or outlandish they might seem.

Evaluate the alternatives

The time for weighing up the alternative solutions is *after* they have all been listed. Even at this stage each person must avoid proposing an alternative as the solution — for having done so, you will feel morally obliged to defend your proposal. It is far more effective first to write down the pros and cons of each alternative.

Joy and I had been discussing a particular problem over a period of months, without coming up with a solution. Every time one of us proposed a solution the other one would point out some disadvantage in the proposed course of action. When we finally got down to listing all the alternatives with their pros and cons, we discovered that each alternative had some disadvantage. With great relief we decided on the solution with the smallest disadvantage, knowing that for us this was the best solution, even though it had some drawbacks.

The couple who experienced conflict in the area of love-making resolved their problem in a rather unique manner. The conflict arose when she told him not to *ask* her to make love, since his obvious disappointment and irritation when she didn't feel up to it, made her feel a failure.

They started off by listing two alternatives. Either he initiated the love-making or he waited for her to initiate it. From this they identified further alternatives. If he initiated the love-making she could
- refuse
- agree reluctantly
- agree willingly.
If he waited for her to initiate the love-making she could
- initiate it
- do nothing.

They then listed the outcome of each of these alternatives. If she refused, he would feel disappointed and she would feel a failure when he showed his dissatisfaction. If she agreed reluctantly he would feel humiliated (more about this in part five) and she would feel resentful. If she agreed willingly it would be great for both of them. Similarly if she initiated the love-making and he responded, it would be enjoyable for both of them. If she did not initiate the love-play he would feel frustrated, and if he showed it, she would again feel a failure and initiate it unwillingly.

Having analysed the situation, they both agreed that *he* should initiate the love-making. They also agreed that the worst outcome for both of them would be for her to submit reluctantly. He therefore agreed that when she didn't feel up to it, he would accept this readily, and not try to exert any pressure on her. In time they began to experience an harmonious sexual relationship, free of stress.

That's all very well, but ...

The win/win approach is one that works effectively in most cases. The problem is that in the heat of an argument when emotions are inflamed, nobody is calm enough to follow this objective procedure. That's why couples *must* agree to call for a truce until they have both calmed down. Walk out of the house — refuse to discuss it further, *but* always let your partner know that you are ready to discuss it later on — otherwise the walking out will be seen as a get-my-own-way technique.

In a nutshell

- — Declare your desires — use "I" messages
- — Resolve the differences on a strict "we versus it" basis
  - • obtain all relevant data
  - • list all alternatives
  - • evaluate the alternatives
- — Always attack the problem, not the person
- — Postpone the discussion the moment emotions come to the fore.

This win/win approach requires self-discipline and concentrated effort but the results are a thousand times more rewarding than the consequences of all the other approaches to handling conflict.

What if ...?

Let's assume that a couple have followed these guidelines carefully and are *still* unable to reach consensus. What then? God gives us very clear answers. The wife must accept and support the husband's decision *fully*. But the husband must make the final decision in loving consideration of his wife (Colossians 3:18, 19). This invariably leads to a strengthening of the relationship.

Kneecap session

Remember the conditions

1. Sit on upright chairs with kneecaps touching
2. Make sure that you will not be disturbed (unplug the phone)
3. Don't attack and don't defend — simply declare and listen
4. Postpone the discussion if it becomes too emotional.

Ask each other these questions

1. What is my typical style of handling conflict? Illustrate with as many actual examples as possible.
2. What is my typical response to your specific style of handling conflict?
3. What are some of the typical illogical thoughts that I express rather frequently?
4. What issue is currently a source of conflict between us? Let's follow the sequence of the win/win approach to resolve this conflict.
5. Let's think of a conflict we've experienced in the past. How could we have handled it according to the win/win approach?

Part 4
Communicating

Check your mate

A closed book

I have often used the words "but why?" when Joy reacts in a way that I do not understand and she has many a time thrown up her hands in exasperation and said, "I'll never understand you men." Why is it that, despite many years of living together, marriage partners still fail to understand each other at times? Why is it that one's partner still remains something of a mystery? One obvious answer is the differences in temperament. A choleric finds it difficult to understand the emotions of a melancholy. A phlegmatic cannot fathom some of the sanguine's impulsive reactions. But there is more to it than that. I think the greatest reason is the lack of effort to try and understand our partners — and it *does* require effort.

Most of us would prefer to be understood, rather than to understand, for real understanding requires hard work, determination and patience — and it is a never-ending task.

The lifeblood of a relationship

Communication is undoubtedly the key to understanding another individual. No relationship can develop and grow without meaningful communication — especially not a marital relationship. When intimate communication dies, the relationship dies — and when the relationship dies, we too die, as individuals. For instance, case histories have shown that infants who had all their physical needs met, but who were deprived of interpersonal contact, developed serious physical illnesses, and even died — simply because they were unable to "communicate" with another person. Patients at a mental hospital are often unable to relate meaningfully to others — in fact, in many cases the lack of meaningful communication led to their hospitalisation.

When communication in marriage ceases we stop growing as individuals. Yet it is estimated that 86% of marital breakdowns are caused by a basic lack of communication. Aubrey was 21 years old and had been married for 10 months. She had just returned to her mother for the second time because she felt that she was being destroyed as a person. She was losing her self-confidence, her zest for life, her spontaneity — all because her husband wouldn't talk to her. Her appeals to "discuss it" and her plea that "we can't go on like this, we've got to talk it out", simply fell on deaf ears. She was right — they couldn't go on like that and so they separated.

A business colleague mentioned to me the other day that for the past two weeks his wife had left a book lying on her bedside table with the title "Talk to Me". He was wondering if his wife was trying to get a message across. We all experience a need for intimate communication with our partners.

Rate your understanding

How well do you really know your partner? Below is a questionnaire which both you and your partner should answer separately.

Every question is asked twice, once relating to the wife and once to the husband. Please answer both questions. In other words you answer the question as it relates to yourself, and you supply the answer your partner is bound to give. Give as much detail as possible, but don't spend too much time thinking about it. Your first responses are the most significant. Do not discuss your answers with your partner until you have both answered the entire questionnaire. Write your answers on a separate sheet of paper.

"Check your mate" inventory

1. What temperament characteristic does the wife consider to be her strongest point?
2. What temperament characteristic does the husband consider to be his strongest point?
3. What temperament characteristic does the wife consider to be her weakest point?
4. What temperament characteristic does the husband consider to be his weakest point?
5. What does the wife fear most as regards the future?
6. What does the husband fear most as regards the future?
7. What is the wife's greatest long-term ambition?
8. What is the husband's greatest long-term ambition?
9. What skill does the wife consider herself to be best at?
10. What skill does the husband consider himself to be best at?

11. What frustrates the wife the most?
12. What frustrates the husband the most?
13. What is the most obvious characteristic that the wife has inherited from her parents?
14. What is the most obvious characteristic that the husband has inherited from his parents?
15. What would the wife like to see changed most in her husband's behaviour?
16. What would the husband like to see changed most in his wife's behaviour?
17. How does the wife want her husband to express his love for her?
18. How does the husband want his wife to express her love for him?
19. What needs of the wife does her husband not meet at present?
20. What needs of the husband does his wife not meet at present?
21. Who had the greatest influence on the wife before she was married?
22. Who had the greatest influence on the husband before he was married?
23. In what area is the wife developing spiritually?
24. In what area is the husband developing spiritually?
25. What is the wife's greatest stumbling block towards spiritual growth?
26. What is the husband's greatest stumbling block towards spiritual growth?
27. How would the wife describe her sexual relations with her husband?
28. How would the husband describe his sexual relations with his wife?
29. What does the wife enjoy most about the marriage relationship?
30. What does the husband enjoy most about the marriage relationship?
31. What aspect of her behaviour would the wife like to improve?
32. What aspect of his behaviour would the husband like to improve?

33. What aspect of your marriage relationship do your close friends admire most?

When you have both completed the questionnaire, please compare your answers with those of your partner and score each item as follows

3 points for answers that were almost exactly the same
2 points for answers that were the same in some areas
1 point for answers that were slightly similar
0 points for answers that were completely different.

The maximum score is 99. Any couple who scored 90 or more, either cheated or are unique as far as their communication is concerned. A score of 70 and higher shows that your communication is at a very high level. A score between 60 and 69 indicates an above average understanding, while a score below 45 suggests that there is much room for improvement.

But we communicate all the time!

A home where real communication has disappeared, does not necessarily mean that partners aren't on speaking terms. In fact a husband and wife can constantly talk to each other, and yet not communicate at a level that creates understanding. They can talk about household matters, relatives, about the children, the neighbours or about a good movie, a newspaper report, or the current fashions. They also communicate often when they argue with each other. But this is not the kind of communication that builds up the relationship and promotes personal growth. Obviously we need to define what is meant by "real communication" — the kind that leads to understanding.

Five levels of communication

In his book "Why am I afraid to tell you who I am?" John Powell identifies five basic levels of communication

1. Cliché conversation
2. Reporting facts about others
3. Expressing ideas and judgements
4. Sharing emotions
5. Peak communication.

Cliché conversation

This is the lowest level of self-communication. In fact we reveal nothing about ourselves and often don't even mean what we say. I have often greeted people passing by with, "Hi! How are you?" and then hurried on without waiting for an answer. Acquaintances who bump into each other by chance will probably say something like, "It was nice to see you again. You must come and visit us some time," to which the reply is usually, "Yes, we will. That will be nice," though neither means it.

A husband may come home after work and ask his wife, "How was your day?" and be only too thankful if she doesn't tell him. We can talk about the weather, or a sporting event or make "small talk" without revealing anything about ourselves. This is the kind of communication one often finds at a cocktail party where people gather only to be lonely together. Telling jokes and funny stories can also be classified at this level. It's fun to laugh together, but not when this is the *main* pattern of communication between husband and wife.

Reporting facts about others

We have a friend who is a very lively conversationalist — yet despite the fact that we have frequent contact with him, we seldom know what is really going on in his mind. Much of his conversation centres on other people, including his family — what they say and what they do, what happened at school, etc. He also relates things that have happened to him, the problems at the office or the time his car broke down, and yet never tells us much about himself, or the things that are going on inside him. When a husband and wife communicate mainly at this level, they may have a great deal to talk about, and yet never expose their inner beings. In fact when people do talk a lot at this level, it is often a way of avoiding communication at a deeper level. Reporting facts and talking about things that have happened is not wrong in itself. Life at home would be extremely dull without this kind of communication. However, if it is the only kind of communication between a couple it is not real communication — the kind that will lead to a deep understanding and strengthening of the relationship.

Expressing ideas and judgements

When we express our opinions and views, we reveal what we *think* about a variety of subjects. We express values and judgements on what is happening around us. For instance, when a couple declare their wishes about handling a conflict situation, they are communicating at this particular level. When a husband expresses appreciation for the way his wife is training the children, he is communicating some of his own values to her. When a wife insists on sending her children to a private school because "they will receive a better education there", she is communicating something of the way she thinks.

Some people, particularly extroverts, are always very quick to express their views and opinions, even when these views are not asked for, while others express their opinions far more cautiously. For example, some people express their judgements in very *general* terms, so that if they meet with any disagreement they can withdraw quite easily without losing face. At this level the individual begins to reveal something of himself and here acceptance by others therefore begins to play an important role.

Sharing emotions

In each one of us is the "real person" — the unique individual we do not often reveal to others. When you talk to me, you may get to know something about me, what I look like, what first impression I make, whether I'm friendly or stand-offish, whether I'm outgoing or reserved — but you will never really *know* me unless I reveal to you the real Arnold Mol. And I can only reveal myself when I share with you my deepest emotions and convictions. When I share with you my hopes, my joys, my indifferences, my passions, my fears, my frustrations, my ambitions — then I'm revealing the things that make me tick, that make me individual. This then is the gut-level communication Powell refers to. This is the kind of communication that leads to being understood — yes, and to understanding oneself, for I cannot *know* who I am until I can *tell* you who I am. This level of communication unites two people intimately. Lack of it causes so many of our emotional hang-ups, stunts our growth as individuals and prevents us from developing our full potential.

When I speak of sharing feelings I do not mean suggesting to your partner, "*I feel* we should buy a new car before the end of the year." Although the words "I feel" have been used, they do not express a deep emotion. Sharing feelings involves revealing some of your innermost being. "When I'm in Frank's company, I always feel inferior because of his sharp reasoning ability," is an example of sharing a real emotion. Just yesterday, a close friend confided in me that he saw himself mostly in a negative light — that he was convinced that others did not have a high regard for him. He did not tell me this to win my sympathy, but to reveal something of what was going on inside of him. He was really communicating.

Peak communication

This can best be described as intimate communion, which makes two people truly one. At such times words may be superfluous, for there is an exhilarating unity of mind, soul and spirit — where I sense that my partner thinks what I think, feels what I feel, experiences what I experience. This is the kind of communication that lifts us above ourselves — that makes us "walk tall" and gives real meaning to our lives. It is a communion and a fellowship that cannot be described — it can only be experienced.

Such communion can rarely be sustained permanently. It comes periodically and can never be planned for. However, the more we communicate at level four, that is the more we share our innermost feelings, the more we communicate our emotions. And the more we reveal our unique selves, the more frequently we will experience these moments of intimate oneness.

Exploring together

The two dimensions of communicating

We can identify a style of communication by plotting an individual's position on two scales

- sending
- receiving.

By *sending* I mean the thoughts and ideas that one person *transmits* to another. The extent to which they do this can range from Low to High. In other words a person whose sending is low, seldom expresses his thoughts or views, while an individual who is constantly talking, displays a high level of sending.

However, communication in its truest form is not simply a one-way transmitting process. It also involves an equal amount of receiving. As kids we used to 'phone each other from a public 'phone booth, without depositing a coin. We knew that the person who made the call could not be heard, but the one who received the call could, so he did all the talking on the assumption that the caller could hear. It was a very strange and somewhat frustrating experience to speak to someone over the 'phone without getting any reply. Yet some people go through life doing just that — mostly sending and seldom receiving.

By *receiving* I mean *listening* — letting the speakers know that we understand their message and that we follow their train of thought. A person who is low in receiving seldom really listens.

Such people may look at you while you speak and even be polite enough not to interrupt, but their thoughts are really either miles away or else they are thinking of what they are going to say next.

Such a person will hear your voice without listening to what you are saying.

At the other end of the scale are the people who listen intently. They show by their responses that they are genuinely interested in what you have to say. They look at you directly and frequently nod their heads or make remarks to show that they follow your line of reasoning.

Communication styles

When we put these two dimensions together, we can also identify five basic styles of communicating.

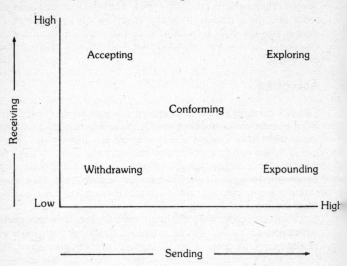

Withdrawing

The person whose communication is characterised by this approach does not say much — perhaps just enough to be accepted in the group. Such people are generally quiet and unnoticed in a social group. They may look at the speaker, but usually show no response to what is being said. They hear but they do not listen. Like the avoidance approach to handling conflict this is an unnatural style, in the sense that very few people, if any, manifest this approach during their courtship days. This style is often acquired in reaction to a dominant partner who is forever expounding his or her opinions, always telling and seldom listening. No wonder their partners learn to "switch off" as time passes.

Some years ago we used to receive an occasional visit from a middle-aged couple. She was a non-stop talker, he hardly ever said anything except "hello", "two spoons of sugar please" and "goodbye". The issue was not whether he would fall asleep during the course of the evening, but rather at what time he would doze off.

Such a relationship is not meaningful. The one partner becomes more and more dominant — the other withdraws deeper and deeper into his shell. In such a home there cannot be a healthy emotional climate and the effect on the children can only be detrimental.

Accepting

This reflects a high level of receiving, but a low level of sending. Such people are marvellous to talk to, and they tend to attract those who have a great need to unburden themselves. They usually make good counsellors, simply because their active listening has such a healing effect on the troubled mind. People who communicate typically in this manner seldom have their own views to get across, with the result that they *accept* more readily what the other person has to say.

In a marriage relationship this can eventually create serious problems. Someone who seldom expresses his or her own ideas or emotions cannot grow as an individual. One sometimes gets the feeling that such a person has no serious point of view at all — that he doesn't believe in anything very strongly. This may lead to a lack of respect. It may also create a sense of unfairness. I know that if I were to constantly express myself and share some of my deepest emotions without my wife sharing something of herself in return, I would feel at an emotional disadvantage — as if she didn't trust me enough to reveal her innermost being to me. On the other hand if my partner always accepts what I say, without ever expressing her own thoughts on the matter, I will begin to lose respect for her intellectual ability, and with time consult her less and less and expound more and more on what's what. Such communication between husband and wife is incomplete and can only lead to an incomplete relationship.

Expounding

Expounders are constantly expressing their own views, ideas, thoughts and plans — often in a forceful manner — without ever stopping to give serious consideration to someone else's point of view, or taking the trouble to listen to other people in order to understand them. When such expounders do listen, it is usually for one of two reasons: they either listen out of politeness (in which case it's more a matter of "keeping quiet" rather than "listening") or they listen in order to expose a flaw in the other person's reasoning so that they can counter it with an argument. Extreme expounders are totally insensitive to their partner's emotional needs. The entire focus is on themselves — what *they* think, what *they* plan, what *they* have experienced. They make no attempt to try and understand their partners, and often interrupt their partners before they can express themselves fully.

I have often been guilty of this. On numerous occasions, when Joy has expressed some doubt or concern about a situation, I have interrupted her and told her that she has nothing to worry about, and that she is just seeing things in the wrong light. I have since begun to realize that such comments only make matters worse, for she began to keep more and more things to herself — to the detriment of our relationship. What she wanted was understanding, not a "logical" argument or an academic lecture. But I'm learning! The other day Joy was rather upset about an awkward situation that had developed when friends had come to visit us. As a choleric I am far less sensitive socially than she is, and I was on the point of telling her that we were not to blame and that it was our friends' fault entirely. This time however, I held my tongue and just listened attentively. I occasionally made a comment, but mostly just gave her my undivided attention. After about 20 minutes she said, "Thank you for being so understanding. I feel so much more at ease now." She turned over and went to sleep. I really felt great, but I also thought of the many times I had tried to convince her to change her perspective — without any success and with a growing conviction on her part that I just didn't understand her.

Conforming

Some people communicate mainly by expressing the views that are acceptable to those around them. They do have views of their own, but they are prepared to adapt them in order to fall in line with what most other people are thinking.

People like this do express their own feelings, but mostly only those which they feel will be accepted by others. For instance, they may tell of the time they arrived late for church when the only empty seats were right in front and how embarrassed they felt at having to occupy their seats in full view of the entire congregation. This was an emotion that was shared — but one that most people would have experienced in a similar situation, and therefore one that would not make them vulnerable to ridicule.

Where the accepter readily listens without saying much, the conformer will listen and then express support. Conformers fit in quite well with most social groups, since they neither dominate the conversation nor withdraw quietly into a little corner. Initially they may express their ideas cautiously to ensure that they are acceptable, or they may listen carefully to gauge the general thinking pattern of the other person or persons. After that, however, they will participate quite actively.

In a marriage relationship this kind of communication can lead to a fairly good understanding provided that both partners are not way out in their thinking and feeling. On the other hand, to continually suppress emotions that are unacceptable, will result in a rather bland and uninteresting relationship. Conformers are usually a little afraid of being different and so they usually communicate in accordance with generally accepted norms.

Exploring

By now you may have noticed that the five styles of handling conflict correspond closely to the five communication styles. The withdrawers tend to avoid conflict. The accepters are likely to yield when faced with differences of opinion. The expanders usually handle conflict in a win/lose manner, while the conformers are inclined to bargain.

The exploring approach to communication is a key ingredient in the win/win style of conflict-handling because the explorer listens in order to understand, rather than to find a weak spot in the other's argument. At the same time the explorer expresses himself fully and clearly so that he can be understood.

Exploring differs from the other styles of communication in quality, and not just in quantity. The explorer does not merely listen more and talk more. His approach to listening is different and he expresses himself differently.

In the first place exploring means *listening* to others

- *with an open mind.* In essence this implies a willingness to learn, and an attitude that suggests, "I want to hear what my partner thinks. He or she may have some views that I hadn't thought about." It means being open to new concepts, new ideas, new perspectives.
- *with an active interest in the sender.* It's more than just "hearing them out" — it's drawing them out. I have often interrupted someone who is sharing an experience, by telling them of a similar experience *I* have had. In the process I was saying that I was not really interested in them — only in myself and my experiences. It also means listening with undivided attention. For instance, when I continue reading the newspaper while Joy is telling me something, I am in fact sending her a message that I'm not really interested in what she has to say.
- *with sensitivity to the sender's feelings.* I don't have to feel what my partner feels, nor think the way she does — but I have no excuse for *not* trying to understand. She gets upset about things that leave me cold — yet instead of telling her "not to be silly" (which neither helps her, nor improves our relationship) I can ask her to tell me about the way she feels, and at least provide a sympathetic ear.

We both learned a big lesson in sensitivity shortly after we were married. While we were driving home one evening I was sharing some very personal matters with Joy. She was listening quietly, but suddenly realized that if we didn't stop then to buy bread, we would have to go quite a long way back to the store later on. So in the middle of my self-revelation she blurted out, "We must buy a loaf of bread." From her point of view it was a perfectly normal thing to say, but I felt shattered. I was baring my soul to her, and her only response was that we needed to buy a loaf of bread. We have since both learned to say something like, "I'm very interested in what you have to say, and I want to continue the conversation — but we need to buy bread, unless you'd like to come back later." This would have left the choice with me, and at the same time conveyed the message that she considered our conversation to be more important.

In the second place, exploring means *expressing* ourselves

- *without embarrassment over our weaknesses*. Joy and I have two very good friends whom we love dearly and whose company we always enjoy. The main reason for our close relationship with Brad and Pep is that we can be ourselves in their presence. No pretence that everything is going well, no presenting an "adequate image", no trying to make a good impression. They accept us with all our shortcomings — and we have always felt free to share our fears, our doubts, our frustrations, yes, even our innermost conflicts with them. It is no wonder that our communication with them is at such a high level.

  In recent years I have told Joy that I feel comfortable with her because I can share my inner self with her, without fear of being ridiculed or told that "a Christian shouldn't think like that".

- *without guilt about our emotions*. As long as we feel guilty about our emotions we can never communicate our deepest feelings in the true sense of the word. We may for example, consider jealousy to be immature, or we may think that fear is a sign of weakness. Doubts may be regarded as lack of faith, or anger may be seen as sinful. As a result we suppress these emotions and in the process hide something of ourselves. Emotions are not to blame — the problem arises when we respond to them inappropriately. It's one thing to feel jealous, it's another thing to forbid my partner to talk to certain men. It's one thing to feel angry, it's another thing to lash out at my partner. We cannot cope effectively with our emotions unless we bring them out into the open. We will discuss this more fully later on.

- *without judging our partners*. Picture the scene. He arrives home several hours late. She has been frantic with worry, imagining all kinds of things that might have happened to him. The moment he walks in at the front door, she lets him have it. "Where have you been all this time? Why didn't you let me know? Couldn't you just think of me for once?" Of course an attack like this leads to a win/lose situation where the husband will either defend himself or counter-attack. How different it would have been if she had said, "I am so relieved to see you safe and sound. I've been concerned that you may have been involved in an accident. I'm glad you're home at last." In this way the wife would be saying exactly how she felt, without accusing her husband and putting him on the defensive. It is vital that we learn to express ourselves *without accusing* our partners in the process.

Exploring means striving to understand and striving to be understood. This is the win/win approach that leads to a high level of understanding. This is the approach to communication that strengthens the relationship and develops us as individuals.

I'm afraid to tell you

We never talk anymore

Time and again I have had a distraught husband or wife tell me
that they no longer communicate with their partners. What they
mean is that they no longer take the time to share their hopes and
fears, their joys and their frustrations. Two days ago Beverley sat
in my study and cried, because after 9 years of marriage she
could no longer get through to her husband. Every time she
pleaded with him to "talk things over" he would promise her that
he would do so, "but not right now". Yet this same couple used
to share so much together in the early years of their marriage.
Now they only communicate frustration, resentment and blame.
Their experience is fairly typical of a great number of marriages.
Somehow the high level of communication that characterises the
courtship begins to decline — for some more rapidly than for
others. With rare exceptions the typical communication pattern in
most marriages can be depicted as follows

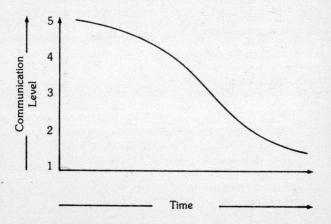

Courtship is usually characterised by a high level of communication. If this were not true, the relationship could not even begin to

develop. Courtship is a time of excitement and wonder as two individuals begin to discover each other. We all grow up isolated in the sense that we keep our deepest emotions to ourselves. However, when we find someone to whom we can reveal our inner spirit, with whom we can share our deepest emotions, whom we can trust with our very hearts, it becomes one of the most exhilarating and thrilling experiences of our entire lives. This is the romance that poets eulogise, authors fantasise and singers croon about. This is the essence of an intimate relationship.

Why the decline?

I want to stress that there will always be a *natural decline* in the level of communication unless a couple take active steps to maintain their communication at a high level.

If this kind of communication is so meaningful, so uplifting, so stimulating, why is there an eventual decline?

Familiarity

One of the major reasons for this decline is the problem of *familiarity*. We assume that we know our partners — that there is nothing left to discover. So we no longer make any effort to explore further. Yet this is a complete fallacy. We will never know all that there is to know about our partners. Every individual has emotional depths that are fathomless — and changing constantly. I am not the person I was a year ago. I have become more mature. I have gained new insights. I have experienced spiritual growth. I have developed new perspectives. What's more, I have a great need to share these changes with someone else — for only then will they really become part of me. Similarly my wife is not the person she was a year ago. She has learned new truths, her reactions have changed, she looks at situations differently, she has gained greater skills and she has developed more self-confidence. She needs to share all this with me in order to discover herself. She cannot *know* who she is until she can *tell* someone who she is.

In the early years of our marriage I thought I really understood my wife, but today, after almost 13 years of being together, I realize that I'm just beginning to touch the surface. It has become an exciting adventure for both of us to rediscover one another.

The thief of time

Another reason for the decline in communication is the lack of time. During courtship most people have considerably fewer responsibilities. Consequently fewer demands are made on their time. In those days a couple could afford to "waste" an evening simply talking to each other. It seems however, that as we become older our lives become just one mad rush. The arrival of children, the demands of a growing career, involvement in extra-mural activities etc. are all given priority. Even our vacations are so filled with activities that we just don't have time to really talk to each other. And unfortunately intimate sharing requires lots of time — it simply cannot be scheduled into a busy programme. "Let's sit down and share — I've got 23 minutes available," will seldom lead to meaningful communication.

Whenever I have to travel some 60 km to Johannesburg, perhaps to speak at a meeting, I take Joy with me if I can — just for the pleasure of being able to talk without any interruptions. When we are alone in the car there are no children demanding our attention, no 'phones ringing, no household chores that need attending to.

It never ceases to amaze me that we always seem to have more time to communicate with our colleagues or our neighbours than we have to talk to our partners. This suggests that we could arrange for time if we really wanted to.

Conflict is another culprit

The third reason for the decline in communication is the way conflict is handled. In the previous section we saw how styles of handling conflict like avoiding, yielding and the win/lose approach, all inhibit communication. Those who avoid conflict neither express themselves nor really listen. The yielding approach also implies that we do not express our own opinions and desires while the strong competitive element created by the win/lose approach would preclude any intimate sharing. Even the bargaining style tends to inhibit people not to expose themselves too much, since this may weaken their negotiating power. Only the win/win approach encourages a high level of communication.

Barriers to gut-level communication

If it is true that 86% of broken marriages fail because of a lack of intimate communication, why don't we all do something about it? Why don't we all make a greater effort to communicate with each other at a level that would deepen our relationship? The problem is that even if we make the effort, set the time aside and avoid negative ways of handling conflict, we still come up against several psychological barriers that make it very hard for us to share our deepest emotions in spite of the fact that we want to. It is therefore important that we recognize these barriers and actively seek to overcome them.

Pride

The major barrier is pride — or inversely a sense of shame. When we share our feelings we invariably expose some of our weaknesses — so our pride often prevents us from doing so. Six months after we were married I was fired from my job. I was so ashamed that I could not tell Joy about it. For a whole week I "went out to work as usual", but in fact I went jobhunting. During that time I experienced a great deal of anxiety about the future, and sharing it with someone would have been a tremendous relief — yet I did not tell her until I had found new employment.

Husbands especially find it difficult to admit their emotional weaknesses to their wives. Men are expected to maintain the *adequate male* image and any emotional weakness suggests a questioning of their manhood. The idealising of the "strong silent type" has not helped to improve a man's willingness to share his fears at all.

People like clergymen, psychologists, teachers and others in positions of leadership find it particularly difficult to share some of their struggles and inadequacies, for fear that they will lose the respect of those who look to them for guidance.

Yet it is when we acknowledge our own shortcomings that we open the way for the other person to share his innermost being. For example, Joy and I have found that when we share our own marital problems with other couples they are more ready to open up to us and in this way they are helped and encouraged to work at their own relationship. In fact when we only present an *ideal* picture, it actually tends to discourage those who are having problems, because they begin to think that there is something seriously wrong with their marriage.

Vulnerability

When we share our deepest longings, fears and ambitions, we make ourselves very vulnerable. We may be laughed at, or ridiculed, or our feelings may be minimised. Joy recently shared some of the frustrations she was experiencing with her domestic servant. Rather than try to show understanding for the problem I tried to show her how she *should* have handled the situation. This didn't help her at all. In fact she felt hurt, and accused me of siding against her. Obviously next time she is going to be far more reluctant to share such frustrations with me, unless I begin to change my responses.

As mentioned previously, John Powell entitled one of his books "Why am I afraid to tell you who I am?" on which one person commented, "I *am* afraid to tell you who I am, because if I tell you who I am, you may not like who I am, and it's all I have." That's why the breaking up of a relationship is so painful — it implies being rejected. And the pain never quite disappears until a new relationship is formed.

We *cannot* experience personal growth without taking the risk of exposing our real selves. It is not very difficult to protect ourselves emotionally, using all kinds of defence mechanisms — but this leads to artificiality and will prevent us from becoming the kind of people that we have the potential to become. We could never be ourselves and life would be a continual coverup — living behind a mask. The result is that those weaknesses, those emotions, those feelings are not dealt with because they are not faced up to — and so they will always be a hindrance to personal development.

Fear of upsetting my partner

Sometimes we refrain from communicating what we really feel because we're afraid it may hurt or upset our partners. We think that it's heroic to "suffer in silence". Sometimes it is confused with the biblical injunction to "bear your own burdens" or "to be the least". A wife may feel that she's expected to keep quiet when she doesn't agree with her husband's plan of action, because she doesn't want to upset him. But that is not submission at all.

The Bible tells us clearly to "speak the truth in love" (Ephesians 4:15). Keeping silent for fear of upsetting our partners can be very harmful.

Recently I heard of a widow who was totally heartbroken because her husband had known for a long time that he suffered from a fatal illness, yet she had only found out a few weeks before his death. She was more upset about the fact that he had not shown his trust by confiding in her than she was about the actual loss of her husband.

Keeping quiet because we don't want to bother our partners with our problems is not an act of love — it is an act of selfishness that will only harm the relationship.

There is another danger in suppressing our emotions for they will find an outlet in more harmful ways. One of the reasons why men suffer more from heart disease than women do may be the fact that men are less inclined to share their frustrations and therefore experience more tension and more inner conflict. Suppressed emotions can also lead to bitterness or self-pity which in turn will have a negative effect on the marriage relationship. The answer is not to keep quiet but to learn *together* how to cope with comments that might possibly upset or hurt our partners.

Self-centredness

Another major barrier to communicating intimately is downright self-centredness — focussing almost exclusively on our own interests and needs. We can be so concerned about ourselves, our own moods, our own emotions, our own ideas, our own plans, that we have nothing left to give to our partners. Each person has a limited amount of emotional energy. The more we spend on ourselves, the less we have to spend on others.

Not only people who always *talk* about themselves are self-centred, but people who constantly *think* about themselves are self-centred too. Shy and withdrawn people are often so wrapped up in their own feelings of inadequacy and fear of rejection that they neither give of themselves to others, nor can they take an active interest in others.

Perhaps this is what Jesus was referring to when He said that the only way to find life is to lose it (Matthew 16:25). I cannot establish a meaningful relationship with another person if I am all wrapped up in myself. Emotional energy that is directed inwards cannot be directed outwards as well. One of the worst forms of self-centredness is self-pity which is a very enjoyable emotion, but a very destructive one — both for the individual and for the relationship.

Self-centredness is simply emotional immaturity — and it has nothing to do with age. A sixty-one-year-old can be just as immature as a twenty-one-year-old, for maturity is related to personal growth and development and not to physical age.

Can we change?

These barriers are not unsurmountable, no matter how serious they may be. Nobody is permanently tied to his past, no matter what the hang-ups might be. The question that faces us is not *"can we change?"* but *"do we want to change?"*

Changing our behaviour — and specifically the communication pattern between ourselves and our partners — is going to take a great deal of effort, patience and courage.

Effort, because it will not happen of its own accord — it must be worked at.

Patience, because we will not succeed fully at the first attempt — we will have to try, try and try again.

Courage, because changing involves emotional discomfort.

There's a real temptation to do nothing — to let things slide, to continue with the same communication style as before. This is certainly much easier. But the price we will have to pay for such an attitude in the long run cannot be calculated — we only know that it will be a very heavy price to pay. For without meaningful gut-level communication we can never grow as individuals — we can only shrivel psychologically. We may achieve power, wealth and so-called success, and yet fail to develop our full human potential. Again the choice is ours.

Telling it like it is

How much do you want to?

Margot had walked out on her husband even though they had been married for less than a year. She was convinced that he no longer loved her, that he didn't really care for her. When she asked me what she should do, I advised her to tell him that she would like to go back, but only if he was willing to see a marriage counsellor with her. When he 'phoned her and asked her to come back because he "couldn't live without her", she told him that she would, but on condition that they attended regular counselling sessions. He was not prepared to do this and one wonders how much he really loved her and whether he wanted their marriage to succeed.

We would all like to enrich our marriages, to improve our ways of handling conflict, to raise the level of our communication. The question is how much do we really want it? Are we serious enough and determined enough to work at it, or will we only try if we can find some short-cut method? Unfortunately there are no magic formulae, no quick remedies, no instant solutions. If we are going to improve our communication it will require effort, patience and courage.

Fight for time

When we have something at heart that we want to discuss or share with our partners, we usually make the time for it. Every now and then Joy makes me sit down and listen to her. It's usually no problem to make time for this kind of communication. However, the most meaningful communication is usually unplanned. We can't schedule it by saying, "When you come back this evening I'd like to share some of my fears with you." To ensure that such communication does take place, we have to set aside time to be alone together. By scheduling such times just to be alone together, we set the stage for deeper communication.

Firstly we must plan this on a daily basis. For instance, set aside the first 15 minutes after homecoming just to share the events of the day with each other. In some households this may be impossible. Then find another time of the day. If you can't, you'd better re-think your priorities. Something will have to go, otherwise your relationship will.

Secondly, set aside one evening a month — or perhaps one evening every two weeks for a fixed appointment that must receive priority over everything short of an emergency. Treat it just as you would an appointment with a V.I.P., for that's precisely what it is. Of course the important thing is to ensure that you have time to talk. Take a walk, go for a drive, dine out, go to a coffee bar, sit in the garden, sit in the lounge, etc. Doing things together like watching a movie or TV can be lots of fun, but it doesn't provide much of an opportunity to communicate.

Thirdly, go away at least one weekend per year — without the kids. This is an absolute must. It doesn't really matter where you go to, as long as you have lots of time to be alone and talk. Joy and I look back on some of these weekends as highlights in our relationship.

Ask someone to stay with your children, or else let them stay with friends. You can even arrange a swop so that your friends can go away for a weekend while you have their children. Where there's a will, there's a way!

Listen to each other

Don't just hear out your partner politely. Listen with understanding. To do that you must first allow them to explain themselves *fully*. So many times I have interrupted my wife, assuming that I knew what she was trying to say, and sometimes I *did* know — but she felt cheated.

Secondly, it is important to ask questions and to encourage them to elaborate further. Ask them what, where, who, when and especially how and why. In the past, whenever Joy said something with which I disagreed, I would immediately come up with some counterarguments. Now I'm working hard at responding with questions like, "Can you give me some reasons why you think the way you do?" When she gives me some good reasons that I may not have considered, I may even change my views. If she can't find any sound reasons, she may change her views. Even better, ask about feelings. The more you ask questions like, "How did that make you feel?" the more you'll be communicating at gut-level.

Another good listening technique is to restate the ideas and feelings your partner has just expressed. A comment like, "If I understand you correctly, you are saying that ...", will either be confirmed or corrected, but always ensure good understanding. Above all, effective listening demands undivided attention. Listening with half an ear while you are doing something else is telling your partner in no uncertain terms what value you place on his or her communication. Occasionally Joy and I have found ourselves getting into a deep discussion while she is preparing a meal. Initially when the conversation was interrupted by food that was ready to be served, we decided that we'd continue after the meal but somehow we never did. Now when we get talking in the kitchen she turns the stove down or switches it off, so that she can give me her undivided attention. Rather an intimate sharing and a late supper than a meal on time with no sharing.

So be on your guard, for you are not really listening when

- you say you understand before your partner has fully explained
- you have a solution before your partner has told you the real problem
- you cut your partner off before he or she has finished speaking
- you finish the sentence for your partner
- you are critical of your partner's grammar, vocabulary or accent
- you are dying to tell your partner something while he or she is talking
- you tell about your own experiences, making your partner's seem unimportant.

The key to listening is not your ability to do so, but rather your determination to do so effectively.

Report emotions immediately

Our emotional problems do not stem from the fact that we experience them, but from the fact that we act on them. It is one thing to feel disappointed, quite another to walk round the house sulking for several days. It's one thing to experience anxiety about the safety of your school-going children, but it's another thing to keep them indoors at all times.

When we act on emotions, especially the negative ones, it can be very detrimental to marriage. No jealous wife has ever kept her husband faithful with nagging accusations — in fact it may be the very thing to alienate him. Nor must emotions be suppressed, for they will find an outlet of some kind — usually a more harmful one, like physical illness.

The answer lies in reporting your emotions at the time you are experiencing them. If you feel anger welling up inside you, don't try to suppress it, it will only cause a burning resentment. Nor should you fly into a rage, for this may have serious consequences. It would be far more appropriate to tell your partner, "Right now, I'm flipping mad."

Obviously it is not possible to report every emotion the moment you experience it — especially when there are others present. However, it is very important to tell your partner how you feel at the best possible opportunity. The more you report your feelings, the less likely you are to act on them or to suppress them, thus avoiding unpleasant consequences.

Be honest

Say what you feel. Report your emotions. Let your partner know where and why it hurts — even if he or she has been the cause of the hurt. The worst thing to answer when your partner asks you what the matter is would be to say, "Nothing." Rather tell him that you're upset, but you can't talk about it right away or you'll burst into tears. Or say that you feel depressed and you don't know why, but your partner is not the cause of this. In this way you're not leaving your partner guessing.

Your negative emotions must be reported honestly and openly even when your partner has been the cause of the way you feel. Always report them in love. Say it in a way that will not be interpreted as an attack or criticism for this will only worsen the situation. Occasionally when I come up with a bright idea and share it with Joy, she sometimes expresses doubts in a way that dampens all my enthusiasm. I once suggested that the two of us spend a long weekend at a seaside hotel. Instead of being excited, she expressed reservations about the cost, what to do with the children, etc. When I challenged her about her pessimism she defended herself by saying, "Surely it's important for me to report my feelings honestly?" Yes, it is important, but we need to be careful *how* we report them. Nowadays, she *first* expresses her enthusiasm and then she starts asking questions!

Honesty is no justification for hurting or condemning your partner. That's why I stressed the importance of "I" messages to avoid the element of personal criticism. If Joy had responded to my weekend suggestion with something like, "That would be fabulous, however, I'm a little concerned about leaving the children behind," it would have had a different effect on me. (That weekend turned out to be an absolute highlight in our marriage.)

State your motives

Explain yourself fully. When I ask Joy, "What time will we have dinner?" she might think that I'm ravenous and want to eat as quickly as possible. As a result, she might feel guilty if there were some delay. However, I might have asked that question because I wanted to get stuck into doing something in my workshop that will require at least half an hour. Had she known that she would have responded differently. It would therefore be far better if I told her my reason for asking.

Avoid "loaded" questions. State your reason for asking. When someone asks me, "Are you doing anything on Friday evening?" I usually reply, "It all depends" — for they might be inviting me to a party, or they might be inviting me to attend a meeting in which I have no interest at all.

More marital arguments are caused by misunderstanding our partner's motives than by any other factor. Tell your partner why you want to do things in a particular way, why you feel the way you do, why you ask the questions that you do. Openness generates openness, while subtlety leads to all kinds of verbal skirmishes. Don't hint at the way you feel, or what you would like to happen. Say it directly. One of the areas of conflict that Joy and I are working through at the moment concerns the amount of help I give her at home, especially when we have guests. I usually become so engrossed in the conversation that I am oblivious to her need for help. She, on the other hand, feels that I *should* be more alert, and offer my help without her having to ask me. She is now working hard at asking me directly — and I'm working hard at anticipating her wishes.

110

Be specific — avoid generalisations

Words like "never" and "always" are usually not true (I was tempted to say "are *never* true"). When a wife says to her husband, "You never show me any affection," she is leaving herself wide open to being proved incorrect, because the husband will probably remind her that several weeks ago he had given her an affectionate hug. It would be much more effective to say something like, "I know that you love me, but I'd like you to remind me of it more often — especially by putting your arms around me more frequently."

Be specific, especially with regard to things that you would like to happen. Many of the words we use are abstract and mean different things to different people. Avoid saying things like, "Please be more understanding," or "loving" or "tolerant". These words are abstract. Instead of using "understanding" you could talk about "helping me think through my own reasoning", or instead of "loving" you could talk about "giving me more compliments when I do things that you like". Instead of referring to "being tolerant" you could ask your partner not to express his or her disapproval every time you make a mistake. These are action words that are specific as opposed to concept words that are abstract.

Please ensure that your non-verbal communication does not contradict your verbal communication. Asking your partner to tell you more about their ideas, while you are yawning your head off will not exactly encourage them to elaborate further.

A good friend of mine recently installed new kitchen cupboards for his wife. He complained to me that same day that his wife was rather ungrateful since she had not even said "thank you". When I had a chance to talk to her alone, I asked her whether she had thanked her husband for the cupboards and she immediately said, "Oh yes, the minute they were fitted." The only explanation for this discrepancy is that she must have thanked him in such a casual manner that it didn't even register.

Beware of the casual "thanks" or the half-hearted compliment. The manner in which you communicate will either add emphasis to what you have to say or contradict it. I have been stressing the fact that it is important to say what you mean, but it is just as important to mean what you say. And this you can only convey non-verbally.

Don't attack your partner

Criticism, fault-finding, condemning, blaming, all lead to win/lose arguments. They are counter-productive, break down the relationship, as well as the individual concerned, and *always* reduce the level of communication.

Express your own emotions in terms of "I" messages, without putting your partner on the defensive. "I feel afraid", "I feel inadequate", "I feel upset", "I feel depressed", "I am jealous", "I am furious", "I am ...", etc. are statements that all explain how you feel. If some of these feelings are caused by your partner's behaviour you can avoid their defensiveness by specifically stating, "I'm not accusing you of being wrong. I only want you to know that these are the emotions I experience when you behave that way."

I cannot stress this enough — *don't judge your partner*. It never accomplishes anything and it will destroy your marriage if you do it often enough.

Don't defend yourself

When your partner shares something with you that may appear to be an attack, don't try to justify your behaviour. Your motives may have been misunderstood or misjudged, but that's not the point. The point is that your partner saw it in a certain light, and that needs to be resolved. Trying to justify your behaviour leads to win/lose conflicts. A far better response is to explore why your partner saw it in the particular light that they did and how such misunderstandings can be avoided in the future.

Defensiveness only reduces the level of communication. Some years ago I bought a house without Joy having seen it. Basically it was a lovely house but there were small things that she didn't like, for example, there weren't enough kitchen drawers. The problem presented itself whenever she mentioned any of these things — I would immediately see it as a criticism of my judgement, and accuse her of not appreciating what I had provided for her. Of course, this was not true — but it upset both of us, spoiling our relationship for a day or two. It would have been far more useful to discuss ways and means of rectifying some of these shortcomings in the house.

Kneecap session

The rules

1. Face one another directly, preferably with knees touching
2. Ensure privacy
3. Don't attack — don't defend
4. Keep the emotional content at a low level.

The questions

1. What is my typical style of communication?
2. What do I do that generally hinders our communication?
3. What are we going to do to make time for ourselves?
4. How can we give one another feedback when our communication is going haywire?
5. Let's go back to our answers on the questionnaire at the beginning of this section and discuss them in accordance with the prescriptions listed thereafter.

Part 5
The key to
happiness in marriage

Happy and unhappy are not opposites

The two dimensions of happiness

If I had to ask you what the opposite of "unhappy" was, you would in all likelihood reply, "happy" — but in a sense this is not really true. If for instance, I were to keep banging my head against a wall, it would make me very unhappy. If I stopped banging my head (i.e. the opposite activity) it would not make me happy. If it did, then the way to find happiness in life would be to bang your head against a wall so that you could stop doing it! And if you wanted to be happier you would merely have to bang your head harder all the time.

That is obviously a silly argument, and certainly not the way to become happy. No, if I stopped banging my head (and I waited for the pain to disappear) it would not make me happy, it would merely make me "not unhappy". That's a kind of neutral feeling.

We often express this in other areas of life as well. When you ask people how they are and they reply, "All right I guess — I can't really complain," they are expressing this neutral feeling. Similarly when my wife brings home a new dress and asks me how I like it, I have one of three alternatives. Either I like it, or I don't like it, or I say, "It's okay," suggesting that I feel neither positive nor negative about the dress. Just neutral.

The same principle applies to casualties. I sprained my ankle some time ago, and it made me very unhappy to have to hobble along painfully. However, the fact that my limbs are in good shape at this moment does not bring me happiness as such. My mobility does not make me happy because that's the normal condition for my limbs to be in.

Similarly the opposite of "happy" is not "unhappy" but rather "not happy" and again it suggests a neutral feeling. In fact there is no difference between "not happy" and "not unhappy" — it's one and the same feeling.

So why all the fuss?

Right now you may be wondering, "What difference does it make?" After all, *the things that make us unhappy do not make us happy when put right.*

This is certainly true in the business world as far as employment conditions are concerned. People can be extremely unhappy about their level of income, but when they receive a pay increase it does not make them happier in their work, it only makes them less unhappy. If I were offered the job of street cleaner at three times my present income, I would probably take the job, but I doubt if I'd ever enjoy it!

In our marriage relationship we experience the same phenomenon. Our partners do things that make us very unhappy but if they were to stop doing them it would not make us happy — it would simply no longer make us unhappy. If a woman constantly nagged her husband, it would probably make him very unhappy. If she stopped, it would not make him happy — it would only make him relieved.

Similarly there are things that make us very happy, but if they were not done, they would not make us unhappy. Occasionally I bring home some flowers for Joy and this always makes her very happy. But when I don't bring home flowers it doesn't make her unhappy. (Unless I forget an important anniversary!)

The two dimensions of marital happiness

In our relationship we can therefore identify behaviour that *prevents unhappiness*, and we can identify behaviour that *promotes happiness*. The question is, which is which!

Behaviour that prevents unhappiness reflects the extent to which we behave in accordance with *our partner's expectations*. Behaviour that promotes happiness indicates the extent to which we meet *our partner's emotional needs*. A friend of ours expressed this most accurately when she said, "I expect my husband to help me with the dishes. If he doesn't I would be very unhappy, but the fact that he helped me this evening didn't make me happy. However, if he had brought me a box of chocolates I would

117

have been very happy, but the fact that he did not bring me a box of chocolates this evening didn't make me unhappy."

What are my partner's expectations?

Some expectations are determined by social roles (although these may be changing). For example, it is normally expected of a wife to prepare the meals. It is usually expected of the husband to see to the maintenance of the house, etc.

Most expectations will depend entirely on the individual couple. In one home the husband may be expected to put the children to bed, in another home the wife may be expected to administer the finances.

There are also expectations as far as the relationship is concerned. A husband may expect his wife to tell him whenever she is annoyed with him, or he expects her to trust him when he's out late, or he expects her to support him in disciplining the children. A wife may expect her husband to compliment her regularly, to share his frustrations and ambitions with her, to take her out to dinner every once in a while, etc.

These expectations do not always have to be in general terms. They can also be very specific for a particular situation. I sometimes have expectations as to how we are going to spend a particular evening, or what we are going to do on holiday. Joy may have expectations of what we will do when friends come to spend a weekend with us, etc.

If these expectations are not met, the partner will feel cheated, and be unhappy and resentful. The problem is aggravated by the fact that many of these expectations are not always expressed clearly or, even more important, are not mutually agreed on. Even if one partner expresses his or her expectations, the other partner may not think them reasonable. They must therefore be discussed *and* agreed on.

I mentioned previously that Joy expected me to help her with some of the household chores without her having to ask me to do so. I felt this expectation was unreasonable. We have since agreed that when she asks, I will help her willingly — and it's working well.

However, merely doing what is expected of you does not bring marital happiness — although in so many homes this is where the focus is placed. Many a man will work long hours every day to "provide his family with the very best" — yet it doesn't make his family happy. In fact his frequent absences from the home are often a source of unhappiness. In the same way, a wife may concentrate on being the best possible housekeeper — running an immaculate household, yet not making her husband happy.

Liz was such a wife. Her home was always spotlessly clean. Her meals always ensured a healthy, balanced diet. Her family was always neatly dressed. Yet her husband left her for a woman who was far more sloppy and unconcerned. What he was looking for was someone who would make him happy — and as a result Liz lost him, even though she had done everything that could have been expected of her. She had, however, failed to meet his emotional needs.

What are my partner's emotional needs?

Although individuals are unique and certainly differ in their emotional needs, we *can* come to some general conclusions about the emotional needs of a man and the emotional needs of a woman.

At this point we need to turn to the Bible to find out what God has to say on the subject. In Ephesians 5:33 we read, "Each one of you also must love his wife as he loves himself and the wife must respect her husband." What does that tell us about the essence of the husband's and the wife's emotional needs?

It tells us that a woman's emotional need is to be loved, cherished, protected and understood. I Peter 3:7 for example, says, "Husbands, in the same way be considerate as you live with your wives and treat them with respect as the weaker partner." The sad thing about the women's liberation movement is that it demands treatment from men which will actually deprive women of having their deepest emotional need satisfied.

The Bible also tells us that a man's greatest emotional need is to be respected, admired and looked up to. That is why in Colossians 3:18 wives are commanded to submit to their husbands — not because they are in any way inferior but because this meets their husbands' deepest emotional needs.

119

Overcoming the curse

In part one I pointed out that God had cursed the marriage relationship because of sin. This curse meant that the woman would desire to control her husband and the man would rule over his wife. Now in the New Testament we read God's prescription for a happy marriage — and it's the very opposite. Instead of wanting to control her husband, the wife must now submit to him. Instead of ruling over his wife the husband must love her to the point of giving himself to her. This is the key to happiness in marriage.

The wife of a happy husband

For women only!

When Joy and I conduct marriage seminars there is only one point where we separate the husbands and wives. This is not because we are about to discuss issues that would embarrass a mixed audience, but for a very practical reason.

A man would be reluctant to put into practice advice on how to make his wife happy if she were present when he was given this advice — for she's heard it all. In the same way her husband's presence creates a built-in resistance — she too would be hesitant to implement advice on how to satisfy her husband's emotional needs if *he* were present when the advice was offered!

In the early days of our marriage I used to read some of Joy's books written for "wives only" — and I know that she was very shy to act on some of the ideas for fear that I might say, "Mmm! I see you're trying out the suggestion on page 53," or something like that. For my own good I no longer read books meant for her only, and she knows it.

In this section I'd like to talk to the wives on how to make their husbands happy, and I want to suggest that if you are a husband, you skip this section and go on to the next one. What's more, tell your wife that you purposely haven't read this chapter — it will give her more freedom to act on the advice.

Don't become a doormat

What does it mean to submit to your husband? Does it mean giving in all the time? Does it mean losing your individuality? No, that's not what God had in mind. Submission does not mean becoming a doormat. Neither does it mean that the wife is in any way inferior to the husband. In fact most wives are superior to their husbands in some way or another.

Submission does not mean that you have to become a slave or a puppet to your husband. The meaning of the original Greek word is "to place yourself under", and what God is commanding wives to do is to place themselves firstly under the husband's authority, so that there is a unity of command in the family, and secondly to place herself under him for the purpose of supporting him and building him up. This is her primary calling as referred to by Dr Louw Alberts in the Foreword to this book.

The authority-submission principle

It always surprises me that people vehemently oppose the authority-submission principle in marriage, although it is accepted in every other aspect of life. God placed the husband in the position of head of the home (I Corinthians 11:3) for only one reason: to ensure good order and to prevent chaos. What would happen in a school where there was no principal or acting-principal? What would happen to a ship that had no captain? What would happen to a hospital without a medical superintendent? What would happen to a business that had no manager? The answer is easy enough: chaos will reign.

Someone has to take the responsibility, someone has to provide the leadership, someone has to make the decisions — and it's no different in the home. God has given that responsibility to the husband — and it's an awesome enough responsibility without having to contend with a wife who is constantly rebelling or seeking to impose her will on him.

Just as in a business situation the manager is not superior to his subordinates (certainly not as a person) so the position of home leader does not make the husband superior to his wife. In fact the wife may have better insight with regard to certain matters than the husband and if he is wise he will consult her and utilise her brainpower. In turn the wife must give her husband the benefit of her insight and judgement. She must not keep quiet. It is only when there is not agreement, that the husband has the authority and the responsibility to make the final decision.

My boss at work often consults me about problems in the firm. On some days we agree and he might follow my ideas — but sometimes he disagrees with me and decides to act contrary to my advice. At that point I have the choice to either support him and to carry out his decision, or else I can resign. *I cannot impose my will on him by refusing to obey him.* True submission therefore is not to leave the decisions to your husband — that's avoidance or yielding behaviour — but to support him wholeheartedly after you have failed to reach consensus. True

submission is therefore to support him in a decision even when
you disagree with him.

The unsubmissive wife

What are the consequences in a relationship where the wife tries
to control her husband and impose her will on him? It will have
one of two effects on the husband. Either he will respond by
establishing a dictatorial rulership, literally crushing his wife emotionally, or he will abdicate his responsibility as head of the house.
A survey conducted by an American university found that
children were happier and better adjusted socially in homes
where the husband was the undisputed head of the family.
Where a wife is exceptionally dominant and the husband particularly withdrawn, there is also a strong likelihood that the sons
will develop homosexual tendencies.
God views an unsubmissive wife in a very serious light. In II
Samuel 6 we read that Michal despised her husband David and
looked down on him. As a result God made her barren for the
rest of her life. In Proverbs 21:19 we read: "Better to live in a
desert than with a quarrelsome and ill-tempered wife." Proverbs
27:15 tells us that "A quarrelsome wife is like a constant dripping
on a rainy day."

What if my husband won't take the lead?

Many a wife has taken over the leadership in the home with the
excuse that "*somebody* has to make the decisions and if he won't
then I'm forced to do so". No doubt a very plausible argument —
but such an approach will not bring about a happy marriage relationship. If a husband does not take the lead in the home the wife
must ensure that she keeps an even lower profile. In other words
she must make sure that she stays "under him", just as God wants
her to do.
Brigitte had a choleric temperament and a phlegmatic husband.
She used to lock up the house at night, she made sure that all the
bills were paid, that the car was serviced, etc. When they had
guests for dinner she would ask one of them to say grace before
the meal. She used to make all the holiday plans and inform her
husband accordingly.

But she wasn't happy, and because she wanted to obey God, she realised she would have to change her behaviour. So instead of blaming her husband as she used to do, she apologised to him for taking over the leadership in the home and announced that from then on she was going to leave the leadership to him.

There was no overnight change and a couple of times bills were left unpaid, while on several occasions they retired for the night with the front door unlocked. However, her husband began to take over gradually. As he took a more active lead, she supported him and expressed her appreciation, which in turn gave him new self-confidence. With time every facet of their marriage including their sexual relations, became a source of real happiness.

God will not hold the wife responsible for her husband's lack of leadership, although He will hold her responsible for her lack of submission. For as long as she insists on taking the leadership responsibility on her own shoulders, her husband will never take over from her. When however, she *does* submit she can leave it safely in God's hands to change her husband.

The working wife

I am not about to suggest that women should not take up employment although much could be said about the harmful consequences on pre-school or young school-going children whose mothers hold down full-time jobs. However, I do want to point out that most working women willingly place themselves under the authority of a boss, and yet some of them strongly resist placing themselves under the authority of their husbands. The working wife has a dual responsibility — i.e. to the boss and to the husband — which may create conflicting demands, or else encourage the wife to assert her independence from her husband, especially since she is no longer financially dependent upon him.

This does not apply to all working wives, but the possibility must be guarded against, for it can become a great source of marital conflict.

The roles of the wife

God created the wife for the very special purpose of being a suitable helper for her husband (Genesis 2:18). As such we can identify five major rules in relation to her husband.

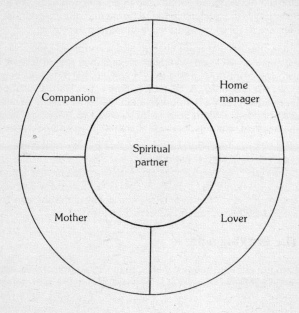

In the rest of this section we are going to discuss what submission really involves in each of these areas, and how the wife can meet the emotional needs of her husband in each of these roles.

Companion

— *Are you fun to live with?* Do you laugh a lot together or does he associate you with complaining? When he suggests doing something or going somewhere do you agree enthusiastically or do you usually express your reservations? One of the things that a woman has to learn is that it is more important to have fun in the swimming pool with her family than to keep her hair in perfect shape. Or that getting all the housework done is not nearly as important as playing games with the family.

What kind of welcome does your husband get when he comes home? An enthusiastic one that says, "Hi, it's great to see you," or is he met by a torrent of problems and complaints? Does your husband look forward to coming home? Occasionally when a wife tells me that her husband is having an affair, I ask her what it is that he sees in the other woman that she might lack. In asking such a painful question I'm not for one minute condoning the husband's infidelity, but rather trying to stress the fact that when a woman meets her husband's emotional needs she need never fear a third party. A third party may not necessarily be another woman, it may be his work or his sport.

— *Does your husband feel "comfortable" with you?* Can he be himself in your company or does he have to mind his p's and q's? Is he free to express himself or does he have to be on his guard in case he upsets you, or gets reprimanded? For instance, a friend of mine is very careful not to mention any other woman with whom he may have been in contact during the day, as this sends his wife into a fit of jealousy. The result is that his conversation with her cannot be natural since he always has to watch what he says.

A woman who is constantly picking on her husband is not fun to live with. There was a time when Joy tried very hard to improve my table manners — without much success. In fact I cured her of kicking me under the table by asking her in front of all our guests why she was kicking me. In time she stopped trying to reform me and just accepted me as I was. Not only did this make me feel more comfortable, knowing that I was not about to be scolded, but I also started making a greater effort to improve my manners!

— *Do you support him when he's under fire?* Whose side do you take when he is involved in some sort of conflict with another person? I used to be very annoyed when I had "near-misses" on the road and Joy accused me of careless driving. It made me feel she was against me. Nowadays she will refer to the other driver as "that reckless idiot" even when I'm the one at fault. And I really appreciate it.

A man can take almost any hammering and face any odds, even when the whole world seems to be against him, as long as his wife believes in him and stands by him. But when she also turns against him and starts pointing out his mistakes, his world collapses for he feels that he has been betrayed.

— *Do you stimulate him mentally?* Perhaps you won't always be able to match his knowledge or hold your own in a debate with him — but then you don't have to. All you need to do is to ask him questions. How will a drop in the gold price affect our economy? What can be done to slow down inflation? What are the implications of the latest political manoeuvres? How will events in the Middle East affect us? etc. etc. Nothing boosts a man's ego so much as when he is asked for his opinion. Just make sure that you ask stimulating questions and listen intelligently. He may not know all the answers, and it may motivate him to do more reading himself. However, in no circumstances must you ask questions just for the sake of asking — then he will feel manipulated rather than respected.

— *Do you involve yourself in his interests?* That does not mean that you have to know everything about motorcars or electronics or what have you. Nor does it mean that you *have* to participate actively in his hobbies and sports. (I really would not enjoy playing squash with Joy!) But you *can* ask questions, and you can show enthusiasm. You might even do some research in a library or talk to a male friend, and then surprise your husband with your knowledge. You can ask about his favourite football team and who the good players and not-so-good players are. Then read about their achievements on the sports page and discuss them with him.

The key issue is your attitude. If you look upon his recreational activities as "a waste of time" or "something that doesn't interest me" you are actually saying that what is so important to him is really unimportant to you and doesn't warrant your attention. He may get the message that you look down on his activities (even if that is not true) and consequently he may exclude you more and more from that part of his life.

Enthusiasm, support and admiration do not require knowledge, insight or participation — just a determination to become your husband's best friend.

Home manager

— *Is your housekeeping an end in itself?* Do you manage your household with the needs of your family in mind, or has it become a showpiece to highlight your own mastery? Janet is a very meticulous housekeeper. The vacuum cleaner is permanently on standby to remove any dirt immediately. The children have to take their shoes off before they may walk into the lounge — and woe her poor husband if he leaves his newspaper lying around, or puts his feet on the coffee table! Her house is not a home — it's just a spotless building.

— *Do you make special meals for guests only?* We would not dream of treating our guests the way some of us treat our partners. Does he ever get a special candlelight dinner with his favourite food? Or is that reserved for guests and Sundays only? I like rice, Joy does not, so when she serves a meal with rice, I get the message loud and clear — she's done this for me. What wouldn't I do for a woman like that!

— *Do you allow him to make the financial decisions?* There is a clear distinction between financial administration and financial decision-making. It's quite alright for a wife to work out a housekeeping budget, pay the bills, etc. But when she also exercises complete control over how the money is to be spent, whether they can afford an article or not, how much to save, what to invest in, etc. she is depriving her husband of a very important part of the home leadership. He should have the final say in all financial matters.

More marital arguments revolve around money than any other topic. A woman who receives a monthly income of her own would be wise to ensure that the spending of their mutual income does not become a source of conflict.

By all means give him the benefit of your insight, but be sure to tell him that the final decision is his and that you will accept it wholeheartedly. By acknowledging his position as head of the home you will actually set your husband free to follow your advice. When however, you oppose him strongly you may actually be "forcing" him to make the wrong decision against his better judgement — for every man has a strong need to prove to his wife that "he's the

128

boss". By submitting to him in this area, you remove the need for him to establish his authority and leave him free to make the best possible decision.

For some wives this may be too risky — but you *can* trust God. When you obey His principles, He will meet your every need. After all, you have trusted your husband with your entire life, so why not trust him with your money?

— *Do you express appreciation for his material provision?* Many men devote themselves wholeheartedly to their work in order to provide their families with a good standard of living. Have you ever expressed your appreciation to him for his hard work and his faithful provision? Do you show your appreciation by spending his money wisely? I mentioned previously that I had bought our home in Pretoria without Joy having seen it, and that there were a number of things she didn't like. She was perfectly correct to point those things out to me — yet somehow it always hurt me, for it made me feel that I had not provided her with what she *really* wanted. Today she loves our home and tells me so regularly.

Wives, I do appreciate that managing a household is not easy and can at times be very frustrating. However, the way you tackle the job can either become a source of discontent for your husband, or it can make him feel he's the most important man in the world, thus meeting his deepest emotional need.

Mother

— *Do you cleave more to your children than to your husband?* The Bible states very clearly that a husband and wife must cleave to each other. Yet it is very easy for a mother to put the needs of her children above the needs of her husband.

Many homes are completely dominated by the activities and schedules of the children. Many a wife has refused to accompany her husband on a business trip, or even go out for an evening because of the demands of the children. However, problems arise when the children leave home and husband and wife have nothing left to share — for over the years they have only related to each other as Mummy and Daddy.

I have always appreciated the fact that Joy has put me first, even when our children were infants, and demanded a great deal of her time. A little while ago I had to speak at a meeting and asked her to come with me. The children were disappointed and asked her to please stay at home and play some games with them. I'm sure that she didn't find it easy, yet she simply reminded them that I would like her to go with me and that it was more important to her. Of course when she feels that she should stay at home on other occasions I readily accept her decision.

— *Do you support him in his discipline? Even when you don't agree?* Since you are at home with the children more than he is, you can either ignore his rules or you can enforce them. I have laid down a rule that our children may only watch four major TV programmes per week. Sometimes Joy would like them to see more, but she has faithfully enforced my rules. If she didn't, she would in fact be saying that I made the wrong decision and that she was not prepared to accept it — with all the negative consequences that would flow from such an attitude. Of course when we are alone she will discuss the matter with me in a win/win manner, but in front of the children she always upholds me as the head of the house.

Be careful that you do not ridicule your husband or run him down in the eyes of the children. Chris was married to an extremely dominant wife, who often insulted him in front of their children. When he shared this with me his greatest concern was that his children had very little respect for him, and this was a tremendous blow to his own self-respect.

Lover

— *Do you make yourself attractive for your husband?* Feminine attractiveness does not depend on the tone of the skin nor on a perfect bone structure.

An unattractive woman invariably displays negative emotions like anger, resentment, fear, anxiety, shyness, scorn or boredom, while most attractive women have an open face, a warm smile, a sparkle in the eye and a warm spontaneity. It is not for nothing that God advises women to concentrate on their inner beauty (1 Peter 3:4) since this is the basis for outer beauty.

What do you do with your hair? Is your style geared to your own convenience or to what your husband likes? Are you attractively groomed when he comes home or does your head look like an explosion in a mattress factory? (I'm referring to curlers in your hair.)

Do you dress to please him or only yourself? Does he like your dresses? Do you ever consult him? A man needs to know that he is uppermost in his wife's mind. And what about dressing provocatively? I don't particularly want my wife to walk around scantily dressed in public, but when she occasionally dresses like that at home just for me, it makes me feel that "I'm the greatest" — and meets a real emotional need.

Do you let him know that he is sexually desirable? Being sexually available to your husband will not make him happy — for it is not the physical need that he wants to satisfy, but the emotional need. When a wife is unresponsive to her husband's love-making it can be an extremely humiliating experience for him. This is his way of expressing his love, and when his wife says "go ahead" but lies there like a dead duck, she is in fact rejecting his love — or at least displaying a total disinterest in his expression of it.

A man is aroused far more easily than a woman — and more quickly. As a result your husband may want to make love more often than you do. Please remember you do not *have* to reach orgasm every time you make love, but you *do* have to respond actively and enthusiastically, if you want to satisfy his emotional needs. At times when you can't even do that, it is better to say "no" than to humiliate him with the "dead duck" routine.

It is also important to initiate the love-making sometimes. More than anything else, this lets him know that you desire him sexually and enhances his feeling of masculinity. Your husband's identity as a man's man is closely linked to his sexual powers. When you disregard that, you hold cheap his manhood.

131

If you admire him as a man, he will have very little need to seek the admiration of other women.

Spiritual Partner

— *Do you allow him to be the spiritual leader at home?* Do you consult him about spiritual problems? Do you allow him to teach the children biblical truths? Do you ever pray together? Does he sense that you look up to him for spiritual guidance, or does he feel spiritually inferior to you? Do you ever ask him to pray for you in times of special need? Do you share your own spiritual problems or experiences with him?
Some of you may say, "I'd love to do all these things but my husband is not a born-again Christian. He does not even go to church with me." In that case the question I'd like to put to you is

— *Does your conduct attract him to Christ?* In 1 Peter 3:1,2, God gives some very specific instructions to wives whose husbands are not believers. "Wives, in the same way be submissive to your husbands so that if any of them do not believe the word they may be won over without talk, by the behaviour of their wives, when they see the purity and reverence of your lives." That's very specific and very practical. The most important command is, don't preach at your husband. Many men have been kept from God's kingdom by wives who have tried everything possible to convert them.
This advice does not apply only to wives with unbelieving husbands. It also applies to wives with Christian husbands. One of the most harmful ways of trying to change your husband is by constantly quoting Bible verses. Not only will it fail to change him, it will also halt his spiritual growth.
There was a time when Joy nagged me to conduct family devotions. The more she put pressure on me the more I resisted, always finding some excuse or other. After a while she stopped trying to persuade me and accepted the situation without any reproach. Not long afterwards I started conducting the family devotions and have been doing so ever since. Why? Because a man will resist being dictated to

by his wife. It's a built-in reaction.

Guard against becoming too involved in church activities. Your first responsibility is towards your husband. If you can participate in the church's activities without any feeling of neglect on his part, then go right ahead. But if he asks you not to go to midweek meetings or not to attend church, then submit gladly — for in doing so you will win him over and you can then both serve the Lord together.

The only time when a wife need not submit to her husband is when he asks her to do something that would violate God's commands directly. Otherwise submit to him as unto the Lord (Ephesians 5:22), willingly and joyfully in *all* things.

You have the husband you deserve

Submission then is not a denial of your identity or a servant-girl mentality. It is an active acknowledgement of your husband as your leader. It is a constant attempt to build him up, to admire him, to respect him. God says in Proverbs 12:4 that "A wife of noble character is her husband's crown, but a disgraceful wife is like decay in his bones." Your husband is whatever you make of him. For you will either build him up or break him down. The more you build him up, the more you will meet his emotional needs — and the happier your relationship will be. The choice is yours! P.S.

Wives should not read the next section. It has been written for husbands. When you give him the book, tell him that you haven't read this section — it will leave him free to take active steps to meet your emotional needs.

Love is not a feeling

What is love?

Husbands are commanded to love their wives. But what does "to love" mean? Is love "not having to say you're sorry", or is it "that funny feeling you get when your eyes meet"? What did God intend when He told husbands to love their wives?

Where do we get our concept of romantic love from? Most of us get it from songs, love stories and movies, and all of these say the same thing, namely that love is a feeling or an emotion that leads to action. There is also the strong implication that it is an emotion that justifies all kinds of behaviour.

A woman once walked into my office and said, "I no longer love my husband." What she meant was that she no longer experienced this feeling of love for her husband, and that she was therefore quite prepared to break up her marriage and to even give up her two-year-old son. Another indication of this belief is the argument men use most often to get a woman into bed, viz. "I love you" — suggesting that love even justifies immoral behaviour.

How does God define love? In the original Greek wording of the Bible, two words were used to describe love: *phileo* and *agape*. *Phileo* can best be described as "affection" and it certainly implies love that involves the emotion. When, for example, Jesus wept at the grave of Lazarus, the people said, "See how He loved him," (John 11:36). Here the word for love is *phileo*. *Agape*, on the other hand, can best be defined as "a unilateral readiness to meet the need of another person". When Jesus illustrated what it meant to "love your neighbour", he told the story of the Good Samaritan who saw a man lying at the side of the road, wounded and beaten by robbers. He dressed his wounds and paid for his accommodation at an inn until he was completely recovered. Now that Samaritan could not have had an affection for the victim, since he didn't know him. In fact he may not even have liked him, especially since Jews and Samaritans hated each other. Yet he acted to meet the man's need — that was *agape* love.

In 1 John 3:16 we have an explicit definition of love *(agape)*. "This is how we know what love is : Jesus Christ laid down His life for us." Again it refers to an action rather than to an emotion. The command to "love your enemies" is *agape* and is decribed in Romans 12:20. "If your enemy is hungry, feed him; if he is thirsty give him something to drink." I find it very hard to like my enemies or to feel affection for them — but I can act to meet their needs.

You don't have to like your wife

Both in Ephesians 5:25 and Colossians 3:19 where husbands are told to love their wives, the word *agape* is used. This means that you don't have to like your wife or even feel an affection for her — but you must act to meet her needs materially, physically, socially and spiritually. That was the solemn vow that you made on your wedding day. You accepted the responsibility for her total welfare — that is your calling which Dr Louw Alberts refers to in the Foreword to this book. You have to love her whether you feel like it or not.

What about the feelings of love?

I am not denying the role of emotions and feelings in love. However, it is not the emotions that lead to behaviour — it is the behaviour that brings about the emotions. And the deeper the need that is being met, the deeper the affection that follows.

Although the Bible does not specifically say so, we can be reasonably sure that eventually the Good Samaritan probably experienced a genuine liking for the man he had rescued. I have often given a lift to a complete stranger. By the time I drop him at his destination I usually experience some feeling of affection for him, however slight it may be. The feeling follows the action.

The Bible confirms this view. Romans 5:8 says, "God demonstrates His own love for us in this: while we were still sinners Christ died for us." This is *agape* love which God gives to every human being, even though as sinners they want nothing to do with Him. When Jesus spoke to His disciples privately He told them that "The Father Himself loves you because you have loved Me and have believed that I came from God," (John 16:27) — here the word is *phileo*. It suggests that although God "so loved the world that He gave His one and only Son", He has a special affection for those who respond to His love and put their trust in

Him. This in turn leads to more loving action. In Revelation 3:19 for example, God says, "Those whom I love *(phileo)* I rebuke and discipline."

As husbands we do not have to experience a feeling of affection before we act lovingly towards our wives — but as we act, so the feelings of love will follow. That means if you want to fall in love all over again, start acting lovingly.

I can't be a hypocrite

Some people have reacted strongly against this approach, saying that anybody who acts contrary to his feelings is a hypocrite. If that is in fact a valid argument, then I must confess that most winter mornings I am a hypocrite — for in getting out of bed I definitely act contrary to my feelings. No, that does not make me a hypocrite — that's merely doing what is required of me — and after a little while I enjoy being up and around and don't want to return to bed. Being a hypocrite is trying to pretend that I am something which I am not. Similarly when I act lovingly towards my wife, even though I don't feel very loving — I am simply obeying God's command.

How must a husband love his wife?

Ephesians 5:25-33 spells it out clearly. A man must love his wife as Christ loved the church. That's the standard. This implies that a husband must
 - put his wife first
 - build his wife up
 - protect his wife both physically and emotionally
 - show his wife understanding
 - provide leadership.

Putting her needs first

Philippians 2:3-5 says we must consider the needs of others more important than our own needs, just as Christ did. This means that as far as *material things* are concerned a new suede coat for your wife must have preference over a new set of golf clubs for yourself, or whatever both of your particular desires may be. In doing this, you are letting her know that she is Number One, and that you take her interests very seriously.

It also means meeting her social needs. As men, we often experience a great deal of *social interaction* in our work situation. We have stimulating discussions with our colleagues and meet interesting people, with the result that *most* of us are only too glad to spend a quiet evening at home.

However, she may feel cooped up at home especially if she has small children, and have a great need to go out — not only with her husband, but also to enjoy male company.

For example, I don't enjoy office parties — Joy absolutely loves them. Similarly I spend a great deal of time conducting business seminars at hotels, so I'm not at all keen on going out to a restaurant for dinner, but she loves it and so I take her gladly. It's always a good investment in our relationship.

We must also put our wives first in our *sexual relations*. Most of us turn on very quickly sexually, like an electric light — and we can make love anywhere, anytime, at the drop of a hat. Women respond differently. They are sexually aroused by atmosphere and romance, and it takes them longer to get warmed up — like an old-fashioned iron. It is therefore very difficult for a wife to respond to a husband who comes home late, reads his newspaper, does some work in the garage, watches a bit of TV goes to bed, and then suddenly puts out a hand in the dark.

Women need to be wooed, some with romantic music, some with low lights and murmuring sweet nothings in her ear — most of them with a time of just communicating together. Occasionally I 'phone Joy in the afternoon and ask her to "switch on the iron" or else when I leave for work in the morning I give her "a kiss with a future". A fun way to prepare for love-making is to have a kneecap session in the bath just before going to bed.

Remember that most women are stimulated by gentle caressing and fondling. The "quickie" seldom satisfies either partner. Women are more easily distracted than men — so ensure complete physical privacy, and give her plenty of time to get everything off her mind. Women are also more easily affected by fatigue than men. Don't force yourself on her if she is too tired — if she has to keep on saying "no" you'll only create guilt feelings in her, and if she gives in reluctantly she'll feel resentful. In either case you both lose. When she does agree to make love readily don't expect her to reach an orgasm each time. Women can enjoy their sexual relations without always reaching a climax — by "forcing" her, you only create a sense of failure in her.

When you put her needs before your own, you are loving her the way God intended you to love her.

Building her up

Proverbs 31 describes "a wife of noble character". One reason why she is such a terrific woman is because her husband praises her (verse 28). Few things have such a powerful influence on a person as a genuine compliment. Every word of praise and appreciation builds a woman up — every word of criticism breaks her down. What's more, we always behave in accordance with what others tell us about ourselves. If, for instance, you constantly tell a child that he is naughty, he will see himself as a naughty child and behave accordingly. I'm not talking about the occasional outburst of the parent, but rather about the continual message that the child receives about himself.

When you frequently tell your wife what a dull cook she is, or what a lousy lover she is, she will become more and more like that. If you constantly pick her out, she will come to the conclusion that she is a failure as a wife, and she will act like one.

However, when you praise her, when you tell her how much you appreciate her, when you frequently remind her of her strengths, it has the same effect on her — and she will begin to act accordingly.

Men often lose sight of the fact that they get their recognition in the work situation — most of us anyway. We accomplish things that we are proud of, we are consulted and looked up to, many of us enjoy some kind of status, we are noticed by others — and this meets a very important need in us. But where does your wife get recognition from? If she doesn't get it from you, she doesn't get it at all. I am convinced that many mothers of young children go back into full-time employment, not so much for financial reasons as for recognition.

In what areas can you praise her? I would suggest five areas where you can begin to look out for things she does well.

— *As companion*. Do you enjoy her company? Is she fun to be with? Do you enjoy talking to her as much as you did during your courtship? Even if your answer is generally "no" then

138

look for the odd occasion when you *do* enjoy being with her
— and then tell her how much you enjoyed her company.

— *As home manager.* Does she spend your money wisely?
Does she cook well? Does she manage the housekeeping
well? How often do you express appreciation for the neatly
ironed clothes in your wardrobe? Is your home attractively
furnished and decorated? Do you take these things for
granted, because it's expected of her, or do you tell her how
much you appreciate her hard work?

I refuse to refer to Joy as a housewife. It has become an
almost degrading expression, especially when a woman
refers to herself as "just a housewife". When I am asked to
indicate my wife's occupation I either put down *domestic
economist* or *home builder* — because that's precisely what
she is. She is not the wife of a house. She is *my* wife, and a
terrific one at that.

— *As mother.* Last year Joy attended a weekend conference
and I looked after our three small children. It was then that I
really began to appreciate what it must take out of her to
mother them day after day. It's not that they are particularly
difficult or disobedient — they just demand a great deal of
attention, as all children do. Sometimes I just wonder how
she manages to cope.

I recognise that the characters of our three children have
been mainly Joy's accomplishment — and I regularly let her
know that she's doing a great job as a mother. I also make
sure that our children express their appreciation frequently.
It's those words of praise that will change your wife's
household drudgery into a joyful task, because she knows
that she is being appreciated.

I also try to meet her emotional needs in this area by occasionally taking the children out on my own, just to give her a
break. Or I bath the baby, and change his nappy when she's
had a particularly heavy day. In each instance these actions
meet her emotional needs, because I'm letting her know
that I care for her welfare.

— *As lover.* Do you ever tell her how attractive she looks? Do
you express admiration for her taste in clothes? Do you
notice when her hair looks particularly nice? In the early
years of our marriage Joy used to make a special effort to

139

look attractive for my coming home from the office. I started expressing my appreciation, and the result was that to this day she makes an effort to look good when I come home. And just reminding her from time to time how I appreciate it, ensures that she continues to do so.

Do you ever tell her that she's a good lover — that she really satisfies you sexually? Do you tell her how sexually attractive she is to you? Women are very sensitive in this area. So many magazines bombard her with the need "to perform in bed" that, unless you reassure her constantly, she may develop an anxiety in this area that will actually prevent her from being a good lover.

Each year Joy becomes more attractive to me. I think her taste in clothes has improved tremendously over the years. Her hairstyle and grooming is always such that I'm proud of her in any company. But I also know that she feels attractive (and behaves accordingly) because I keep on telling her how terrific she looks.

— *As spiritual partner*. Does your wife set the standard for spiritual life in your home? Does she seek to live a godly life and educate the children in the ways of the Lord? Is she an example to you and the children? If so, do you tell her so? Or do you criticise her in other areas because she makes you feel guilty about your own spiritual life? A godly woman can be a man's greatest asset, for she determines the quality of your home life. Don't erode that asset.

Many a woman is frustrated because she feels spiritually alone — either getting no support from her husband, or actually receiving only opposition or disdain. Even if you find it difficult to provide the spiritual leadership in the home, you can at least encourage and support her in this area — and give her recognition for the spiritual standard that she maintains in the home.

Every husband gets the wife that he deserves, for she becomes what he makes of her. If you constantly run her down, you'll end up with a disgraceful wife. If you constantly build her up, you'll have a wife with a noble character. Proverbs 12:4 says, "A wife of noble character is her husband's crown, but a disgraceful wife is decay to his bones."

The choice is yours as to what kind of person your wife will develop into.

Protecting her

1 Peter 3:7 describes the wife as "the weaker partner" and as such she needs to be protected. Most of us have no difficulty in acknowledging the fact that we are to protect our wives *physically*. Not many of us, however, recognise that she needs *emotional* protection even more.

- *From the children*. A mother's nerves can be run ragged by children. Disobedience, back-chatting, cheekiness, etc. all take a heavy toll on your wife's emotions. She needs your protection. In our home I will not stand for any hassling of Mum. If the children do not obey her instantly, they know that they will have me to reckon with in a way that doesn't leave much room for debate. Cheeking Mum is met with swift reprisal. Constantly nagging her, or yelling for her to come is simply not allowed.

  Recently we visited some friends in the evening. When it came to bed-time the four-year-old boy didn't want to go. The mother had to speak to him several times, without receiving any response. Finally she dragged him off to his bedroom screaming — somewhat embarrassed by our presence. During this whole scene the husband merely looked on, and in so doing failed to love his wife. There must be no doubt that the father is head of the house — but the children must have no doubt whatsoever that in the father's absence, his authority has been fully delegated to the mother.

- *From the in-laws*. Why are most of the in-law jokes about the husband and mother-in-law, and very few about the wife and mother-in-law relationship? Could it be that the latter is so often a source of conflict, that it is too serious to be joked about? Some months ago a husband asked me to come and talk to his wife because *she* had some serious problems. It turned out however, that his wife was being totally destroyed by *his* mother and that he was doing nothing to protect her. His mother would come for a visit and promptly start re-arranging the furniture, make critical remarks about the neatness of the house, point out her daughter-in-law's inefficiency, and in fact openly suggest that her son would do well to divorce his wife. At first I couldn't believe it that a mother-in-law could do such things, but he admitted this to be true. He had failed to protect his wife and the marriage relationship suffered untold damage as a result.

I remember that when our first baby arrived, Joy was a bit apprehensive because my mother was coming to stay with us for a few weeks. As my mother got out of the car, I greeted her, then took her to one side and said, "Mum, remember it's óúr baby. We're glad you've come to stay, but I'd appreciate it if you didn't offer any advice about the baby unless Joy specifically asks you." To this day I'm not sure whether I upset my mother or not — but my first responsibility was to protect my wife.

— *From difficult decisions.* The burden of decision-making can be rough on a woman's nerves. Shield her from this. Make the decision for her. I strongly believe that the ultimate responsibility for the family finances rests with the husband, and you should not abdicate that responsibility to your wife. By all means consult her and involve her — but *you* must accept the responsibility for the final decision.

There is no way that you as husband can justify the abdication of your leadership role in the house — and that means especially the decision-making role. There are obviously many decisions you can and should leave to your wife, especially with regard to managing the household, but whenever a particular decision causes emotional stress for her she should be able to delegate it to you.

— *From fatigue and time pressure.* In our home we refer to the period between 17h00 and 19h00 as the "Valley of the Shadow", and I think this is probably true of every home with young children. That's the time when the kids are tired and become difficult, while Mum is flustered in the kitchen trying to get dinner ready on time. That's when her nerves are sensitive and her fuse very short. That's when she needs emotional protection more than any other time. That's when you need to step in and bring order into the chaos. Keeping the kids away from her at that time may be a greater act of love than all your caressing in the bedroom.

— *From tense relationships*. Although a husband probably cannot protect his wife from every awkward situation, he can nevertheless make sure that she is not constantly burdened by tense relationships. She should, for example, not have to get involved in a drawn-out wrangle with a shopkeeper about a defective article that she wants to return. Nor should she have to be troubled by difficulties with neighbours or relatives.

Once an incident at a neighbour's house led to some hasty and somewhat unkind words being spoken. Joy felt upset about this, since the neighbours were good friends of ours. I considered it my responsibility to go to the neighbours and clear the whole matter up, thus protecting Joy from having to cope with this tense situation.

On another occasion a great misunderstanding arose between her and her mother in the course of their correspondence. Although Joy does virtually all the letter-writing in our home, I had to put pen to paper and clear up the situation. Again it was my responsibility to protect her emotionally.

Understanding her

The fourth way in which a husband is to love his wife is to be sensitive to her moods and feelings. 1 Peter 3:7 also says that husbands are to "be considerate as you live with your wives". The word "considerate" can also be translated "according to knowledge", and it suggests understanding them and accepting them.

This means accepting their moods and emotional fluctuations. It means taking the trouble to listen to them — to be sensitive to their needs. It means learning to express love in their language — rather than in your language. And in their language, love means tenderness and gentleness.

It has taken Joy quite a few years to put some romantic notions into my head. I always considered things like flowers, little love notes, special greeting cards or a slab of chocolate as "sentimental rubbish". But I'm learning, and it never ceases to amaze me what a tremendous return on investment I get from the money I spend on a bunch of flowers, or a single red rose, not to mention things like opening the car door for her, walking on the right side of her in a busy street, and generally treating her as I did when we were courting. An occasional 'phone call in the middle of the day just to say "hello" also works wonders. Ian Webber, the well known marriage counsellor, told us of a husband who was often away on business trips, but always 'phoned his wife at 19h00. This did not impress her at all, and she accused him of only thinking about her five minutes before he called and forgetting about her five minutes after he had hung up! Later in a private conversation, Ian advised him to 'phone her in the middle of the day. The husband reluctantly agreed and so on his next trip about 400 km away from home, he 'phoned her at 11h00 in the morning. When she heard it was him she said, "Hang on, I'll just get pen and paper to write down the message." He had quite a problem convincing her that he did not want her to do anything — that he'd just 'phoned to say "hi". After quite a long conversation he hung up and, on the spur of the moment informed his colleagues that he had to go home for a while and that he would be back in a few day's time. However, halfway home he passed his wife going in the other direction. She too had told her teenage children that she would be away for a few days. They discovered each other all over again.

Loving your wife means trying to understand her — and to do that you must take the time to communicate intimately with her.

Leading her

There are numerous areas where a husband can provide loving leadership. For some it may be with regard to disciplining the children, for others it may be guidance on how to deal with the domestic servant. One wife may need help with household budgeting, another may need direction with regard to the kind of Christmas gifts she should buy for the family. Whatever the need or the situation is, a husband must provide leadership in the areas where his wife needs help most.

Above all, he needs to be the spiritual leader in the home. The Bible states clearly that "the husband is the head of the wife, as Christ is the head of the church" (Ephesians 5:23). If you abdicate this responsibility there is a breakdown in the authority structure that God instituted for the home — with many negative consequences, not only for the marriage relationship and your own personal development, but also for the children who grow up in that situation.

Do yourself a favour

One last thought on the matter of loving your wife. The two of you are one – whether you like it or not. So every time you run her down, you run yourself down. Every time you build her up, you build yourself up. Every time you love her, you love yourself. No woman will be able to resist being loved the way I've suggested in this chapter. Her response will be to love you, to look up to you, and to meet your every emotional need. No wonder then that the man who loves his wife is only doing himself a favour.

Just one word of caution. If you suddenly bring her some flowers, or start complimenting her, she may get the fright of her life. Depending on her temperament she will either ask you, "What do you want from me?" or she will want to know what you've been up to.

Changing your typical behaviour is not easy and some men have tried to do it very gradually. But that doesn't work very well. A more effective approach is to tell your wife that you've read a book that has made you realize how little you do to express your appreciation for her — and that you've bought her some flowers (or whatever) just to tell her that she's a fabulous wife.

I accept no responsibility for the consequences of her reaction!

An impossible standard

I'll never make it

If right now you're feeling that the standard expected of you is too high and that you'll never be able to live up to it, you're quite right. To expect a wife to submit to her husband as unto the Lord, and to expect a husband to love his wife as Christ loved the church, is simply expecting too much. It will require a superhuman effort to achieve that — and since we can't see ourselves achieving that standard, what's the use of trying? The built-in tendencies to the contrary are a major reason why it is an impossible standard. As we see in Genesis 3:16, there is a natural inclination for a wife to want to control her husband and for a husband to want to lord it over his wife. What it therefore boils down to is that God expects us to act contrary to our natures. That's exactly what He expects — and since He knows that we cannot do it by ourselves, He has given us His own Spirit to enable us to obey Him. The entire passage in Ephesians 5 dealing with husband-wife relationships is preceded by a command in verse 18 to "be filled with the Spirit". The question is, how?

God's standard

What must one do to be acceptable to God — to be righteous in His sight? The answer is found in Matthew 5:48: "Be perfect therefore, as your heavenly Father is perfect." This means that the only person good enough to come into God's presence is the person who has never sinned. Hebrews 12:14 says that, "Without holiness no one will see the Lord."

Well, that rules me out for sure! For I am a sinner and all my efforts to earn God's favour are as filthy rags in His sight (Isaiah 64:6). I will never be able to be perfect. But God knows that and because He loved me, He came in the person of Jesus Christ, lived a sinless life on earth and then died on the cross to pay the penalty for my sin. In so doing He conquered death and provided a way of salvation.

The answer

Now for the good news. God says that when I put my trust entirely in Him, He will make me perfect in His sight — and not just for a little while, but forever. Hebrews 10:14 says, "By one sacrifice He has made perfect forever those who are being made holy." II Corinthians 5:21 says that He will give me His own righteousness — that means that as far as God is concerned I am as perfect as Jesus Christ. I do not understand this fully — but I believe it because He said so.

Secondly, when I put my trust in Him, He will give me His Holy Spirit to enable me to live a "supernatural" life — a life where I am not bound by my sinful nature, but where I am free to obey Him. In II Corinthians 1:22 we read that "He anointed us, set His seal of ownership on us, and put His Spirit in our hearts as a deposit, guaranteeing what is to come."

Thirdly, He will give me eternal life. It is not something I *hope* to get one day — I may *know* that I have it, for in 1 John 5:13 we read, "I write these things unto you who believe in the name of the Son of God, so that you may *know* that you *have* eternal life." If God says so, I'll believe it.

How will I know?

The Bible tells us that there are two indications that we have been made righteous in His sight. The first is the assurance we have in our own hearts. Romans 8:16 says, "The Spirit Himself testifies with our spirit that we are God's children." (It may surprise some people that not everybody is "a child of God". We can only become children of God when we accept Him as Saviour — John 1:12.)

The second evidence is a desire to turn away from sin. 1 John 5:18 says, "We know that anyone born of God does not continue to sin." Linked to this is a desire to obey Him in our daily living.

The love triangle

There is a third party in our marriage — The Lord Jesus Christ. He lives by His Spirit in both my heart and Joy's — and He has made all the difference to our marriage. At the time of our courtship most of the people who knew us, expected our marriage to end on the rocks — because we were such extreme opposites. And in the first few years we had tremendous adjustment problems.

But as both of us consciously started obeying the Lord with regard to submitting and loving, our relationship changed radically for the better. We came to understand that God never gives a command without also giving the ability to obey Him. This didn't happen overnight. It was and still is, a process of growing and learning together. And we trust that this process will never stop as long as we're on earth together.

An open invitation

We are by no means a special couple. We have many friends who also enjoy a great marriage relationship because they too, walk in obedience to God's commands. God's invitation is open to all. In Luke 11:13 Jesus says, "How much more will your heavenly Father give the Holy Spirit to those who ask Him," while in John 6:37 He says, "Whoever comes to Me I will never drive away." This is therefore available to all.

Eternal life is not something you can work for. It is a gift from God that can only be accepted (Romans 6:23). Whether you accept or reject His gift is up to you.

I am, however, convinced that this is the starting point for many couples who are serious about renewing their marriage relationship. I can think of no sounder foundation to build on than to invite a third party — Jesus Christ — to share your love relationship. He is the only One who can truly make your marriage different — the way you wanted it to be. With Him as your Captain, you can both win.